IAN HAMILTON Collecte

Ian Hamilton was born in 1938, in King's Lynn, Norfolk, and educated at Darlington Grammar School and Keble College, Oxford. In 1962, he founded the influential poetry magazine, *The Review*, and he was later editor of *The New Review*. He also wrote biographies and journalism, mainly about literature and football. He died in 2001.

Alan Jenkins has published six collections of poetry, of which the most recent are *A Shorter Life* (2005) and *Revenants* (2013); he was poetry critic for the *Observer* and the *Independent on Sunday* from 1985 to 1990, and is deputy editor of the *Times Literary Supplement*.

also by Ian Hamilton

Sixty Poems

IAN HAMILTON
Collected Poems

Edited with an Introduction by
Alan Jenkins

faber and faber

First published in 2009
by Faber and Faber Ltd
Bloomsbury House
74–77 Great Russell Street
London WC1B 3DA
This paperback edition published in 2013

Typeset by Faber and Faber Ltd
Printed in England by T. J. International, Padstow, Cornwall

A CIP record for this book
is available from the British Library

ISBN 978–0–571–29534–0

FSC
www.fsc.org
MIX
Paper from
responsible sources
FSC® C101712

10 9 8 7 6 5 4 3 2 1

Contents

Introduction

'So far as they can be said to be famous at all, Ian Hamilton's poems are famous for being small in size and few in number': thus Dan Jacobson began his subtle, admiring contribution to a Festschrift published for Hamilton's sixtieth birthday. The latter's *Sixty Poems* also appeared at the same time, adding ten new poems, all short, to *Fifty Poems*, published ten years earlier. Hamilton would have been seventy-one this year. In the three years between the publication of his last volume and his death at the age of sixty-three, he published two further poems. Given seven more years he might well have managed another collection: a *Seventy Poems*.

He had ruefully acknowledged the unprolific nature of his poetic gift in the moving, matter-of-fact preface he wrote for *Fifty Poems* in 1988:

Fifty poems in twenty-five years: not much to show for half a lifetime, you might think. And, in certain moods, I would agree. In certain moods, I used to crave expansiveness and bulk, and early on I had several shots at getting 'more of the world' into my verse: more narrative, more satire, more intelligence, and so on. Each time, however, I would end up knowing for certain that I could have tackled the material more cogently in prose. Why push and strain?

And so I decided to stop thinking like a poetry pro, to stop fretting about 'range' and 'output'; decided, indeed, to keep the whole business of 'my poetry' quite separate from the rest of my so-called literary life: a life of book reviews, biographies, anthologies and magazines. I suppose I thought that I would wait for poetry to happen rather than force myself to go in search of it. After all, the poems I *had* written arrived more or less out of the blue, prompted by circumstance rather than by any subject-seeking impulse on my part.*

The inspiration for those poems may have arrived 'out of the blue', but the poems themselves left little to chance. The circumstances that prompted them were 'upsetting' ones, as he later put it: his father's death from cancer when Hamilton was thirteen, and his first wife's mental illness. The stakes were as high as they could be. 'Did I truly

* See Appendix 3 for complete preface.

think that poetry, if perfect, could bring back the dead?' Hamilton later asked himself. 'In some way, yes, I think I did.'

Hamilton's first collection, *The Visit*, was published in 1970, though some of the poems in it date from 1961 or '62, when he was in his early twenties. He had been writing poetry since a bout of scarlet fever in his teens led to the discovery of a 'so-called heart problem', and his removal from the football pitch. A sickly figure, 'banished to the library during games', he said, 'I reached for my Keats. Keats was pre-eminent. You know, half in love with easeful death . . .' All his life Hamilton maintained, only half-jokingly, that football was where the 'real poetry' was. He did not play, at least not competitively, but, he said, 'You should see me *watch*.' His team was Tottenham Hotspur: a lonely and often unrewarding passion, as he admitted, but one that would not let him go.

'A so-called heart problem'; 'my so-called literary life'. Hamilton was anything but a so-called poet, however. He was, rather, 'a poet who was also a critic, an editor and a biographer, and it was his search, in all of these places, for "the real thing", as he put it, which earned him much of his distinction'. So begins Hamilton's entry in the *Dictionary of National Biography*, written by his friend of many years, Karl Miller, and the unhesitating way in which 'poet' is placed first among Hamilton's vocations, though undoubtedly right, may surprise some. The brief entry for 'Hamilton, Ian' in the *Oxford Companion to Twentieth-Century Poetry*, which he edited, very properly restricts itself to listing some of his publications (including verse) without further comment. On his death, more than one obituarist regretted the loss of the best *prose* stylist of his generation. And by now there is probably another whole generation of readers who know Hamilton not as a lyric poet at all, but as the author of an outstanding Life of Robert Lowell (1982), or as the defendant in a lawsuit brought by J. D. Salinger, the subject of the biography he wrote next. (Salinger objected to some quoting from personal letters, freely available for inspection in university archives, and sought an injunction; Hamilton cut the offending quotes, re-wrote the book, and was mortified. The author of *Catcher in the Rye* had been a hero of his adolescence, and 'phoney' remained one of his favourite terms of disapprobation.)

Others will have known him as a book reviewer and critic, whose hundreds of reviews, essays and articles take twenty-two small-print pages to list in his bibliography; or as the author of a book-length meditation on the artistry of the Spurs and England footballer Paul Gascoigne. Still others, no doubt fewer in number, will have read his stylish study of *The Little Magazines*, his tour around the literary estates in *Keepers of the Flame*, or his sometimes caustic thumbnail summaries of forty-five modern reputations in *Against Oblivion: Some Lives of the Twentieth-Century Poets*; he also edited several anthologies and the *Oxford Companion* mentioned above. Before or during all of this activity he was 'Special Writer', then Poetry and Fiction Editor on the *Times Literary Supplement* (1965–72), and Editor of *The Review* (1962–72) and *The New Review* (1974–79): a flinty-eyed scourge of poetasters and pretension, a witty, sardonic pillar of the Pillars (of Hercules, a pub in Soho), and, among women, a handsome, Bogartian figure with an intriguingly complicated private life.

When Hamilton's *A Gift Imprisoned: The Poetic Life of Matthew Arnold* appeared in 1998, some detected a poignant personal subtext in this account of the Victorian poet-sage's gradual abandonment of poetry – or its abandonment of him – for the drudgery of school-inspecting and other good works. Certainly, Arnold's 'Dover Beach' was a touchstone for Hamilton: a left-over Romantic poem, and one that spoke to his own sense of being a left-over romantic. He admitted to having been powerfully moved by this passage from Arnold's notes:

It is a sad thing to see a man who has been frittered away piecemeal by petty distractions, and who has never done his best. But it is still sadder to see a man who has done his best, who has reached his utmost limits – and finds his work a failure, and himself far less than he had imagined himself.

And Hamilton's own predicament does haunt several passages in his book, such as this: 'What the age didn't need were more poems of the kind that Arnold did have a real gift for, and had indeed already written: lyric poems of the self, that Arnold self which, as he came to believe, had or should have had better things to do than, well, write lyric poems.'

Hamilton may have had many *other* things to do than write poems, but he would not have agreed that any of them were better things. 'Miraculous lyrical arrivals' he called the poems he did write, and, given his so-called literary life (or, as he put it in even less self-forgiving mood, a life spent calculating 'all the crappy things I'd have to do if I didn't do this crappy thing'), the miracle would seem to be that they arrived at all. At the very least, their rarity and brevity might seem unsurprising. But that would be to confuse the poet with the busy man of letters, or with the bohemian who took up his station in the saloon bar next door to *The New Review* offices, ready for the next round – and the next round of critical hostilities. Poetry, though it was 'revelation' rather than 'something constructed', was also a painstaking and profoundly moral business. Hamilton's poems, among the most heartfelt of their time, are also among the most reticent: they are, in the best sense, modest. This reticence or modesty is central to understanding both the man and what he thought poetry could and should be. Blake Morrison, writing ten years ago, put it succinctly when he said that writers 'move between two poles: self-expression at one extreme, self-effacement at the other. Though not as violently as Salinger or Matthew Arnold, Hamilton has himself struggled between these same poles.'

Hamilton was born in 1938, the second son of Robert Tough and Daisy (*née* McKay) Hamilton, who had left their native Scotland in 1936 and were living in King's Lynn, where Hamilton senior worked as a civil engineer. In 1951 the family, now increased by a third son and a daughter, moved north to Darlington, Co. Durham, and Ian attended the grammar school there. After two years' National Service, stationed in Germany with the RAF (Information Service), he went up to Keble College, Oxford, in 1958. At Oxford the young Hamilton, 'tough, austere, unprivileged, unpretentious', as his friend and fellow-undergraduate John Fuller has described him, quickly made his mark on the poetry scene, his 'tight-lipped authority' already fully formed. As a poet, though, he was still feeling his way, equally unimpressed by torrid 1940s neo-Romanticism, by Dylan Thomas's bardic posturing and by the preening ironies – a kind of parade of diffidence – that were *de rigueur* in the Movement-dominated 1950s.* In fact, his undergraduate poems clearly owed something to the cool, tough-guy stance of the Movement's youngest member, Thom Gunn; but of Keats, anyway, there was no trace. On the evidence of one or two surviving items of juvenilia, he had been ousted even earlier, by T. S. Eliot and Wilfred Owen:

> What waits beyond the terror and the dirt,
> And the teacup-tinkling laughter and the talk,
> The smiles around the mouths of savage men? . . .
> If the lie is spent, the salutes should cease
> [*etc.*]

When the seventeen-year-old Hamilton wrote these lines, in 1955, the Second World War was only ten years in the past. For many – combatants and civilians – who had lived through that war, understatement or some form of stoical holding-back had become essential coping mechanisms. In 'Not Another Dedication', written for Hamilton after his death, Peter Dale, another Oxford contemporary and friend, invoked

> Something ingrained in our war-child years:
> tears were the thing to fight against
> when drained of every other strength.

(See, too, Hamilton's own 'Veteran' and note.) By the time he reached Oxford, Hamilton had probably already encountered the poems of Keith Douglas, whose sangfroid and 'neutral' tone, as Hamilton later called it, plainly made an impact. (Not long after, in his essay 'The Forties', he analysed the rather different 'self-detachment', 'necessary if one is to keep sane', to be found in the poetry of Alun Lewis. This essay, and an anthology edited by Hamilton, *The Poetry of War 1939–45*, presented Douglas, Lewis and Roy Fuller as the pre-eminent poets of the war.) Here, perhaps, was a version of the more brooding 'unspoken' which sometimes weighed heavily on the Hamilton household.† Feelings, anyway, were to be kept manfully in check.

* See Appendix 2.
† See the note to 'Father, Dying', pages 92–4.

At the same time, poetry was no good without them. What was wanted was something with the craft and discipline of Movement poetry but without its 'notable aridity'. In later years Hamilton described the crucial importance to him of 'feelingful' poems by Anthony Hecht and Theodore Roethke, of *Heart's Needle* by W. D. Snodgrass and *Life Studies* by Robert Lowell, both published in 1959: 'To me these books, these individual American poets, came as revelations.' What had drawn him to 'half a dozen' of Lowell's poems at that time were the personal subject matter, the passionate speaking voice with its 'heartbreak note', 'teetering above sentimentality without falling into it'; while the 'internal rhymes and basic iambic line broken up into highly disciplined free verse sounded like somebody really talking'.* By 1962 Lowell was being championed by the influential A. Alvarez as a poet who exemplified a much-needed 'new seriousness' to combat the 'English disease' of gentility, a poet prepared to 'face the fact that he is moved, whether he likes it or not, by forces that are very difficult and very destructive'. Sylvia Plath, admired by both Alvarez and Hamilton, added her approval in a BBC radio talk: 'I've been very excited by what I feel is a new breakthrough that came with, say, Robert Lowell's *Life Studies*. This intense breakthrough into very serious, very personal emotional experience, which I feel has been partly taboo. Lowell's poems about his experiences in a mental hospital, for example, interest me very much.'

Now Lowell's voice would help to release Hamilton's own. But there were important differences. The autobiographical poems of *Life Studies* are for the most part artfully candid, first-person accounts of family drama, marital tension and mental breakdown, rich in circumstantial details of the poet's life and the lives of his relations and intimates. In his essay 'A Biographer's Misgivings' Hamilton touches more than once on Lowell's controversial outspokenness, and he returned to the subject in the conversations with Dan Jacobson that he recorded in the last year of his life. 'Lowell was a confessional poet, a writer who had gone beyond customary bounds of reticence or personal embarrassment.' And again: 'By the early 1970s there was nothing that Lowell would *not* say in a poem.'

* For more on the importance of Lowell's free verse, see Appendix 2.

For Hamilton this kind of detailed self-examination and out-spokenness were neither possible nor desirable. The perfect poem, he told Jacobson, had to contain 'the maximum amount of suffering'. But it also had to contain 'the maximum amount of control'; and the suffering should not be the poet's suffering, but someone else's, albeit someone close to him. 'It wouldn't be about me; rather, it would be about my inability, however intensely I felt, to do anything about the suffering . . . One didn't want, on the other hand, to sound wimpishly hopeless about it.' His own poems – spare, undemonstrative, full of anguished tenderness and claustrophobic unease – favour 'you' or 'your' over 'I'. Speaking 'to' his dead or dying father, to his mentally ill wife, the poet is in both cases (and in both senses) recalling them, bringing them back to life or to mind. Like all lyric poets, he is more or less talking to himself – another 'you'. His only two insistently first-person poems – 'Complaint' and 'Bequest' – are dramatic lyrics spoken by, respectively, the widowed mother and the dying father. The others are 'ideal speech', 'the perfect thing to say to this person at this time – if they were alive or capable of attending'.

At the same time, a poet 'must always be suspicious of making poems out of suffering which is someone else's'. Hamilton could not, for example, condone Lowell's inclusion, in his late poems, of un-altered or barely altered passages from letters written to him by his second wife when he abandoned her – though it's true he also thought the poems in question 'weren't any good'. For himself, 'I am express-ing very private emotions as if to another person. But I have no right to make that person's real-life suffering public . . . I was speaking to someone who couldn't answer back.'

The pained awareness that his solicitude comes too late or falls on deaf ears puts these poems in a direct line from Thomas Hardy's 'Poems of 1912–13', written after the death of Hardy's first wife and full of, as well as tender remembrance, sorrowful acknowledgement of his own failures or neglect while she was alive. And Hamilton's concern for the subject's right to privacy makes for a poetry that is, for all its indebtedness to Lowell and other American exemplars, not just self-effacing but self-denying. The poems contain very little information about the everyday lives or identities of the people in them. The reader is a kind of eavesdropper on the moment of crisis or climax in a personal drama. Interiors – bedrooms, sickrooms, hospital rooms – are no more than implied; a countryish, perhaps suburban out-of-doors is evoked with highly selective precision. (To Jacobson, Hamilton admitted having 'a rather melodramatic or pinpoint visual sense. One thing strikes me.') Apart from the odd, startling touch of *chinoiserie* or *japonaiserie* – brevity is not the only Imagist contribution here – there is almost no individualised description. (Those aestheticising touches in fact tend to blur rather than sharpen the dying man's identity, and that of his mourners.) Too much description, Hamilton said, 'might seem like a poetic *relishing* of the situation'. The real issue was: should he be writing about this at all?

Later Lowell made Hamilton uneasy because his refusal to censor himself often caused damage in his life – damage which would in turn provide the subject matter for more poems. Just as Hamilton qualified Lowell's line from 'Epilogue', 'Yet why not say what happened?', with 'You want to say what happened, but not necessarily who it happened to', so the poems of his own middle years (and there was to be no opportunity for a late flowering) revisit familiar scenes and relive familiar unhappiness in search not of poetic capital but of emotional salvage. They hint at unspoken regret for things done or undone, lives not lived or lived badly; they touch glancingly, ironically on precedents in literary careers such as Edmund Wilson's ('Was it not dolorously fitting that he should find himself, at forty-five, serving the creativity of an old college chum whom he habitually viewed with condescension?', Hamilton wrote about Wilson's mission to rescue F. Scott Fitzgerald from oblivion). They attempt to acknowledge whatever – light, love, happiness – has 'managed to get through'. Perhaps reflecting the much greater part that was being played by fiction and biography in Hamilton's life as a reviewer, biographer and editor, they let in slightly more of the world, more detail, more description or evocation. As in earlier poems of Lowell's such as 'Home After Three Months Away', the impulse to confession in them, far from a straightforward unburdening, encompasses the hope of forgiveness, healing or repair.

What was it that had done or was doing the damage? A clue was provided by Hamilton himself when he wrote about these later poems that, although they were written from the heart,

I'm not sure that my heart was *in* much of what I got up to in these 'trashy years' – from about 1973 to 1979. The raggedness of everything, the booze, the jokes, the literary feuds, the almost-love-affairs, the cash, the somehow-getting-to-be forty . . .

Poetry, then, had more than ever to be kept apart, protected from the worldliness of the poet's everyday existence. The booze and jokes would become the stuff of legend, and of magazine journalism ('An Alternative Agenda' contains intimations of Hamilton the boon companion, but he knew his gifts were not really for 'light' verse of this kind, and he did not reprint it in either *Fifty* or *Sixty Poems*). The raggedness, the almost-love-affairs, the literary feuds and the cash – 'the trouble with money' as Hamilton called it, the trouble being that he hardly ever had any, and never kept it for long when he did: these are all very much part of the hinterland of his poetry after *The Visit*, and that poetry's peculiar melancholy, the melancholy of tarnished dreams and troubling responsibilities, survival and counting-the-cost.

Hamilton had always been preoccupied with the question of how a writer should live: in a poet's case, how daily life could be reconciled with obedience to 'the Muses' sterner laws'. At least part of the fascination of his biographical writings lies in his search for examples or models – or warnings. His own sparing 'output' of poems was not of the kind to attract the honours, grants and prizes which have eased the lives of many poets in the post-war world, and he knew it. In Stephen Spender, he seems to have found a compelling anti-type: the Establishment man of letters, circumambulating the globe from conference to committee meeting to cultural jamboree. Even if Hamilton never *settled for* anything, he knew what it meant to do so, and inevitably he responded warmly to the poems of the librarian Philip Larkin: to 'Mr Bleaney' especially. (In widowhood Hamilton's mother had supported the family by taking in paying guests, and later there was a brief period when Hamilton himself felt too close to Bleaney's circumstances for comfort.) In *Against Oblivion* he quotes Larkin on the subject of Edward Thomas: '"One cannot help thinking that

Thomas was that unfortunate character, 'a man of letters', to whom no humiliation or hardship outweighs the romance of scraping a living from the printed word"', and adds, 'of course, "romance" is the key word. Just as Thomas saw the romance draining from his once splendid love of [his wife] Helen, so he witnessed the erosion of his youthful fantasies about the "literary life".'

Though this should not be taken as a statement of Hamilton's own case, it is revealing all the same. The 'so-called literary life' he *did* live, though it barely provided him with a living, was – as one of his obituarists pointed out – all the life he craved. There might have been, in this, a touch of puritanism inherited from his Scottish parents, or 'something ingrained' during his wartime childhood and the years of post-war austerity. In *Writers in Hollywood* he explored the lives of those who had sold out in some way, who were 'unable to cleave to the high road'. His own youthful fantasies, clearly, cleaved to that road. 'It was Mammon vs. the Muses', he recalled much later in his essay 'The Trouble with Money'. 'Back when I started, insolvency spelt glamour. There was a near-priestly romance in the idea that a high-purposed literary career would be profitless, at least in terms of cash.' Puritan and dreamer seem to meet in that 'near-priestly romance'. In reality it could not be sustained for long. On the one hand, to have a mortgage was contemptible; on the other, 'a fellow ought to be able to pay for the next round', without stooping to Dylan Thomas-like indignities. Not having achieved a good enough degree for a career in academe, Hamilton hit on a novel compromise: starting a poetry magazine. (Or so he saw it in retrospect. But before *The Review* he had produced *Tomorrow*; and before that, at school in Darlington, *The Scorpion.* 'The little magazine virus', according to John Fuller, 'raged untreated in Ian's blood.')

Sending off a new issue to the printer to reassure him that he would be paid for the previous one, Hamilton made *The Review* a byword for critical fearlessness, encouraging it in his contributors as well as practising it himself. 'The texture, always dangerously thin . . . wilfully chopped up, undramatic . . . superficial rhyming . . . arbitrary seeming . . . the general drift towards prose', etc.: in these terms Colin Falck, in *The Review* no. 2, chastised Robert Lowell – the same Robert Lowell whom *The Review*'s editors thought the most important poet writing in English. Adopting the pseudonym 'Edward Pygge', Hamilton could have fun at his subjects' expense; of Ned O'Gorman, for instance:

Toweringly pretentious, intricately boring, and painstakingly derivative, [he] unleashes his clichés with an effrontery that can only be termed: 'rare' . . . The poems stand, defying all attempts at interpretation or justification, almost begging, it would seem, to be ignored.

'I'd feel, *You call this poetry?*': thus Hamilton summed up his early crusades in an interview with Gerry Cambridge in 1996. He would come to look back with a certain amount of self-irony on his youthful absolutism, an absolutism reinforced by the conviction that a bad line was 'a crime against nature'. 'I'm prepared now to concede that there might be various kinds of excellence in poetry, some of which I'm blind to. I felt then that there was only one sort – which I was custodian of,' he told the same interviewer. Yet the confidence and seriousness that fuelled *The Review*'s stringencies were remarkable, and the stringencies themselves remarkably even-handed. True, the tone was more acerbic when it came to 'legitimate targets', 'popsters and barbarians' such as the Liverpool poets: 'They were getting praised and enjoyed. They had an audience. There was a sort of Leavisite/ Arnoldian feeling, that the Philistines were at the gate,' Hamilton said, many years after the event. Not unduly hampered, in his criticism, by his otherwise highly developed sense of the rights of others, Hamilton (also, by now, reviewing regularly in the *London Magazine* and the *Observer*) set about making enemies.

Some of them were still enemies when he started the more lavish and ambitious *The New Review*; and this new magazine made other enemies besides, many of whom were motivated by envy or exclusion. Most of the best and best-known writers of its (and our) time were published in it. But, while it had its complement of poets, including some carried over from *The Review*, it would be more celebrated for its discovery and promotion of prose-writing talent. By now (the mid-1970s) Hamilton had lost his appetite for the poetry wars. And there was the usual trouble with money – in fact even more trouble, since, thanks to Arts Council subsidy, there was more money. 'It was completely mad,' Hamilton told Gerry Cambridge. 'We started out very grandly paying contributors. We ended up borrowing money from *them.' The New Review* achieved much in its fifty issues before the bailiffs moved in – in 1979, the year of Margaret Thatcher's first election victory. The bigger battle, against consumerism, mass communications and the 'flood of mediocrity', was now a losing one. The Philistines were no longer at the gate; they were swarming all over the citadel.

Retrospectively, again, Hamilton could be valiantly self-romanticising about the 'failure' of this particular dream: 'I liked the idea of being up against it, on the run and in the right.' Privately, he would admit to feeling that he had 'lost whatever it was we set out to achieve' – lost in more than one sense. Poetry was supposed to be a message in a bottle from a culture 'shipwrecked' by money; perhaps it could even hold back the tide. Now everything seemed to have been engulfed. And the career he had subsequently taken up, that of biographer, might even have made him complicit in the draining away of poetry's prestige. Biography, he saw, by offering readers a way of 'possessing' a poet, also provides an excuse not to bother with the poetry; or plays into the hands of Philistines by giving them 'something to use against the work they don't anyway want to read'. The weariness, the wry acknowledgement of defeat, in most of Hamilton's poems of the 1980s ('Larkinesque', 'The Forties', the unpublished 'Untranslatable'), remains personal, but a note of Arnoldian cultural lament can just be heard through the sadness, the 'late acknowledged bewilderment' and the foreboding in poems such as 'House Work', 'Again' or 'Dream Song'.

'Dream Song' borrowed its title from the celebrated sequence by John Berryman, who had rivalled his friend and contemporary 'Cal' Lowell in poetic invention, and outdone him in determined self-destructiveness. But it was Lowell's particular way of excess with which Hamilton, as his biographer, became more personally involved. As he told Dan Jacobson, he was often appalled:

What's at issue is the idea of a life given over to creativity; and the belief that because a person believes himself to be possessed of some profound and special gift, he has certain rights to live his life in a certain way. I suppose the real question is: what price do such persons pay and what price does the world pay for this gift which they think they have, which they claim to have, and perhaps do have? Lowell seemed alarmingly and repugnantly, overweeningly, to believe that he was a great poet, so he thought he could do pretty well what he liked.

In Salinger, too, 'there was a sense of specialness, a sense of *I am*'. For both these writers, and for many close to them, the price paid had been high. 'Great poetry might get written about madness, but there is no such thing as great madness,' Hamilton noted on the very first occasion he wrote about Lowell, in 1963. From the vantage-point of the 1990s, he looked back unenchanted (though with perhaps the merest hint of nostalgia) to what he called 'the glamour of poetic instability', to the days when 'the best American writers were crazy, drunk or dead by their own hands'. He heartily disliked the new dispensation according to which writers 'are expected to project themselves as cool, well-organised achievers, just like everybody else'. But he also instinctively recoiled from the attention-seeking self, the tyrannical *I am*. He had witnessed enough of it – in poets, in his own private life – to know the damage it could do.

Keepers of the Flame looks at the way some writers go on claiming attention beyond the grave, and even controlling what kind of attention they receive: managing their own immortality, or ensuring its management by 'flunkeys, acolytes' – and widows. Even before the Salinger case, Hamilton had learnt some hard lessons about the morality and politics of biography. In the 1960s, writing his introduction to the *Selected Poetry and Prose* of Alun Lewis, he realised that Lewis had probably killed himself while on active service in Burma, but Lewis's still-living widow and mother were understandably 'committed to the idea' that his death had been an accident. With Lowell, there had been many affairs, and there were *his* widow, his ex-wife, his children and his mistresses to consider. The opportunity existed, here, to do even more damage. 'So what do you do? Tell the truth or bear in mind their feelings?' Hamilton's priority as a biographer was the truth, but other people's priorities mattered too.

And what if the biographer's work amounted to nothing more than 'snooping'? A brilliant chapter of *Keepers of the Flame* makes Henry James's ambivalence towards biography into a paradigm. For all his love of mystery, of the inscrutable ('the artist was what he *did* – he was nothing else'), his shudders of distaste at 'vulgarity and publicity and newspaperism', James could also acknowledge the 'supremely natural' nature of biographical curiosity. Hamilton had himself become, through a combination of disposition and necessity, one of the 'new style inquisitors', but one who was well aware of what James called 'the whole question of the rights and duties, the decencies and discretions of the insurmountable desire to *know*'. As a biographer Hamilton remained very close, in this respect, to the poet who carefully weighed his responsibility to the subjects of his poems. And somewhere behind both was the thirteen-year-old boy who sat at his dying father's bedside through weeks of what he later called 'service'.

From that came what amounted to a belief: that what a virtuous life would be about would be caring for somebody else. I think my mother made all of us feel very responsible for her welfare after he died . . . She'd been left on her own with this terribly hard life . . . And then in my marriage it became clear that I had married a sick person, a person who was going to be ill repeatedly and probably for ever, so there was this continuity with what I had felt throughout my adolescence: this was what life's about. And with that maybe came the wish for a controlled structure: you had to keep your control however bad things were; you had to be in charge.

'Possibly I exist or only feel I exist', he continues, 'when I am called upon to serve or assist or something. Otherwise I don't really have a personality, an existence.' For anyone with such a feeling, most poetry – perhaps poetry *per se* – would probably look like an indulgence. It might look less like one if, in its controlled structure, in its decencies and discretions, it could become something like caring for somebody else, or at the very least, one area where that remained possible.

This almost certainly played a part in the appeal, for Hamilton, of poets such as Alun Lewis – 'The Depression, plus a high-minded literary mother, shaped the essentials of Lewis's always pressing sense of duty. From early on, though, he had trouble reconciling his dreamy, introverted personality with the ruder practicalities of public service' – and Keith Douglas, whose father had left home when he was eight: 'His mother was his chief confidante: she was sickly and impoverished but staunchly genteel . . . Keith in turn saw himself as both dependant and mainstay, as stand-in for his absent and unmentionable dad' (both as seen in *Against Oblivion*). Above all, it played a part in his eventual reckoning with the shade of Matthew Arnold, whose far-from-absent and much-mentioned 'dad' dominated his son's life.

Arnold stopped writing poetry when he reached the age at which his father had died, in his mid-forties. This, and the tension between Arnold's sense of social responsibility and his irresponsible, lyric self, the feeling in some of his poems that 'he was running counter to something', fascinated Hamilton, who was in his early fifties when he began to contemplate writing Arnold's biography. His own dad had died at fifty-one. When he reached the same age Hamilton visited his father's grave in Darlington and was, he wrote in an unfinished essay, painfully aware of absence ('Today, for the first time, I had the feeling that he *wasn't there*. He had become more dead, or dead and gone') and of being somehow delinquent or disloyal for 'going on ahead', into unknown territory, or at least territory unknown to Hamilton senior. 'I went up and stood beside his grave', Hamilton told Gerry Cambridge, 'and did a second goodbye, and thought: *now what? Now what?*' His last poems, ominous, otherworldly, owe much of their power to a sense of disorientation, of lost bearings as well as lost years. In more than one of them he seems to inhabit his own afterlife.

'I think I feel', Hamilton had written when he was fifty, 'that if you are a lyric poet of the "miraculous" persuasion, then you will never properly "grow up". There won't *be* a middle period of worldliness and commonsense – or if there is, you won't know what to do with it, in verse.' Poems such as 'The Garden' and 'Responsibilities' suggest, though, that it might take a poet almost a lifetime to know 'what to do with it, in verse' – 'it' this time being the most important dream of all, 'the imaginable moral power of perfect speech' to which Hamilton refers in his life of Lowell. Just what he meant by that he made clear in a conversation with Peter Dale published in 1993:

Say that the subject of a poem is the suffering of another person. I think I believed that by writing the poem, there might be some mitigation of the suffering. One knew that in life ordinary speech made little difference, couldn't save the other person from death or from illness. Poetic speech might work differently ... While writing a poem, one could have the illusion that one was talking in a magic way to the subject of the poem. One might even think that this was doing some good, making things better.

Though, he went on, 'of course, you know it isn't. You wake up and it hasn't', this was one dream Hamilton never relinquished, one no worldliness or common sense could touch, no matter what else had, bafflingly, changed.

And much *had* changed. According to Hamilton's near-contemporary Hugo Williams, 'it would be hard to exaggerate the influence Ian had on the way poetry was written in the Seventies'. Now several decades have passed, it would be hard to exaggerate the extent to which that influence has waned. In part, this has to do with fashion, with inevitable changes in what we want from poetry and poets. (If we want anything, that is. 'The poet,' as Hamilton put it in the 1990s, 'if he has any sense of his own importance, it's a huge sense, of being the central figure of the tribe, the seer, the wise man . . . Yet the facts tell him that he's of no consequence at all.') Hamilton saw the way things were going when he came to write the introduction to *Fifty Poems* in 1988. Twenty years later (and forty years after the heyday he was looking back on), expansiveness, bulk and range are highly valued commodities, the poetry pro reigns supreme and the poet is less a seer than a licensed entertainer, no longer mad or drunk but tamed and tenured and spruced up to teach remedial creative writing. Hamilton's withdrawnness and intensity, the way poetry, 'by his practice of it', became 'not craftsmanship or profession but catastrophe' (as Michael Hofmann put it), his insistence that, a really good poem being almost impossibly difficult to write, most poets will never write one: none of this was going to be exactly welcome in the all-shall-have-prizes world of 'outreach' or the poetry workshop's cheerful, can-do ethos of co-operative endeavour. (Not that he didn't have a go: there was more than one short stint as a poet in residence, but the title, and the role that went with it, didn't seem to take.)

Then there was his voice: not just 'the emotional climate we like to call "voice"' but his *voice*. During his interview with Dan Jacobson Hamilton recalled a brief period spent (see above) at Hull University, which brought him into contact with Philip Larkin: 'He was immensely tall and very deaf. I don't speak loudly, so I could never be sure he heard anything I said. We used to go and have a beer in the bar, and I've really no idea how much he heard.' 'I don't speak loudly': in fact he spoke precisely, laconically, wittily – and extremely softly. And the 'voice' in his poems rarely rises above a tentative whisper. It has not been difficult for other voices, louder, more insistent, more hectoring or simply more indulgent towards the supposed needs of the audience, to take up the available space, let alone the 'space' for readings. (Reading his poems to a roomful of strangers was close to torture for Hamilton, and he was never going to be a popular or successful figure in a world where 'it's the day-to-day expectation of poets that they spend two-thirds of their time reading their poems aloud in village halls or wherever'.)

Living poets' reputations depend not just on readings but on publishing, frequently or at least regularly – which Hamilton showed an uncommon reluctance to do. After their deaths, for a while at least, poets remain visible by having spawned followers, imitators, a school, and in the 1960s and '70s, school-of-Hamilton poets were to be found in the pages of *The Review* and (to a lesser extent) *The New Review*. But they developed, moved on, or fell silent, perhaps in recognition of the fact that the only successes likely to be achieved by the severely self-limiting Hamilton/*Review* style had already *been* achieved – most of them by Hamilton himself. (Though he does not entirely exclude his own work from the strictures he expressed about that style: see the note to 'Vigil'.) In the Festschrift for Hamilton's sixtieth birthday, several of his (mostly younger) fellow-poets were unstinting in their appreciation of his qualities: 'extreme, and extremely pared-down' but with 'a surprising lushness' (Andrew Motion); 'unyieldingly tender, acidically lyrical' (Douglas Dunn); 'beauty and compression and sorrow', 'tenderness and delicacy and terror' (Michael Hofmann); 'etchings and not, as prejudice once suggested, smudges' (Peter Porter); 'uniquely lyrical, passionate and sorrowing' (David Harsent); 'The laconic lifting into lyric. Tight-lipped. Vulnerable. Irresistible' (Craig Raine). Yet not one of these poets, with the possible exception of Hofmann, shows much trace of Hamilton's influence in his own work, and I can't think of a single other poet who does – or does any longer. In other words: Hamilton's particular 'real thing' was inimitable. It was also irreplaceable, but it has been replaced all the same, by several varieties of other thing, some of which he would not have regarded as real.

From one point of view, Hamilton's apparent lack of concern for his own poetic posterity looks wilful, even reckless, like his daily consumption of nicotine and alcohol. From another, he simply, complicatedly, refused to play the reputation game, to 'fabricate' poems or 'pretend something was a poem when [he] knew it wasn't', or pursue the 'phoney' rewards that greater fame might have brought, even to a modern poet, even after he was no longer around to be embarrassed by them. It looks contradictory, too, in as much as he *did* continue to write poems, almost until his death, and to publish, if sparingly, when he was ready to do so. But that is itself consistent with the other contradictions which, as we have seen, are at the heart of this imposing but softly-spoken, 'feelingful' but very private poet. 'You used to know', goes the phrase repeated like a mantra in his late poem 'Resolve', addressed to a figure whom he calls 'Enchantress, know-all, Queen of Numbers, Muse' and who is both his inspiration and his conscience:

> You used to know how hard I tried
> And how foolhardily I'd swear
> That this time I'd not falter. You could tell
> What lay in store for me, and what I'd spent
> And what might be retrieved.

Hamilton's life, consumed as it was by responsibilities of one kind or another, by damage and repair, spending and retrieving, was nevertheless, at a deeper level, spent in service to this Muse's sterner laws. That buried life is to be found in the pages of poems that follow – graceful, haunted poems, haunting in a way that is out of all proportion to their size, into which he almost certainly believed he had put the best of himself. 'And all', he used to say, 'because they wouldn't let me play football.'

Note on the Text

Faber published three volumes of Ian Hamilton's poetry in his life-time: *The Visit*, in 1970, followed by *Fifty Poems* (1988) and *Sixty Poems* (1998). *Fifty Poems* contained all thirty-three pieces from *The Visit*, with some revisions and in a slightly different order, and a further seventeen written after that first book appeared. *Sixty Poems* reprinted *Fifty Poems*, with the addition of ten new pieces. Before or between these slender books came three even slenderer booklets: *Pretending Not to Sleep* (1964), *Returning* (1976) and *Steps* (1997). In each of these, poems appeared for the first time that would be republished, again with occasional revisions, in the subsequent Faber volumes. Twenty-three poems were included in Faber's *Poetry Introduction 1* in 1969, all of them reappearing in *The Visit* a year later.

Hamilton was scrupulous in his attitude to his own work. His was a small output of – for the most part – painstakingly revised and 'finished' poems. This, together with his publishing history of further revisiting and refinement, means that he left an unusually clear picture of his poetic intentions, of the body of work he wished to preserve and be remembered by. With one exception ('Windfalls'), the poems in the main part of this book are printed in the last versions Hamilton approved – in many cases, this means the same versions he approved on two, three, four or five separate occasions, going back to 1964. They are printed in the order in which he last arranged them, for *Sixty Poems*. This was almost identical to that of *Fifty Poems*, which in turn departed only slightly from that of *The Visit*. ('Family Album' and 'Almost Nothing' were completed after *Sixty Poems* came out, and both were published before Hamilton died.)

The alternative would have been to arrange the poems in chronological order of composition, but the chronology is in many places impossible to establish for certain. With only a very few exceptions, Hamilton did not date his typescripts; a probable date can be suggested for some poems but for many more this remains conjectural. In any case Hamilton's own ordering is highly effective.

The approximate date of composition can be inferred from that of first publication, which is given in the notes. Variants between different published versions of poems are also given in the notes. (There are occasional inconsistencies in punctuation, and where comparison with typescripts, drafts, etc., suggests that these are due to careless proofreading rather than deliberate choice, only the last-published or last-corrected version is given.) The contents of the original volumes, in their original order, can be found in Appendix 3.

The second part of this book contains, as well as a handful of unpublished pieces from all periods of Hamilton's writing life, eight poems that were published in journals (and, in one case, in *Pretending Not to Sleep*; in another, in *Returning*) but not thereafter. Five of these are very early work – all written in 1960 or '61, and published in undergraduate magazines. (They were also typed up and copied on cyclostyled pages used by Hamilton's friend John Fuller, then a lecturer in Manchester, for a course he taught on contemporary poetry; this group originally included 'The Storm', 'The Recruits' and 'A Mother's Complaint'.) These five (along with the unpublished 'The Veteran' from the same period), albeit they lack the power and poise of the poems Hamilton did include in *Pretending Not to Sleep* and/or *The Visit*, so clearly anticipate the voice, the preoccupations and the subject matter that were uniquely his that they merit inclusion here.

Appendix 1 contains, in sequence, the drafts of the unpublished 'Letter to the Editor', which offer a remarkable insight into Hamilton's working methods.

As well as the brief personal lyrics for which, as I have suggested, he would wish to be remembered, Hamilton occasionally (in the persona of 'Edward Pygge') produced parodies of contemporaries, pastiches or satirical squibs. These belong to Hamilton's journalistic rather than his poetic history, but one such poem is printed in Appendix 2, with some remarks made in interview that are revealing of his attitudes to poetic form, and to poets who had been important to him.

Along with the contents of his original volumes, Appendix 3 reprints Hamilton's only published commentaries on his own poems: on *The Visit*, from the Bulletin of the Poetry Book Society, No. 65 (the book was the PBS Choice, Summer 1970); and the original preface to *Fifty Poems*.

Acknowledgements

I am very grateful to the following for their help and advice: Al Alvarez, Jamie Andrews (Curator of Modern Manuscripts, British Library), David Barnes, Stephanie Cross, Peter Dale, Michael Fried, John Fuller, Gisela Hamilton, Matthew Hamilton, Judith Hesketh, Michael Hofmann, Mick Imlah, Dan Jacobson, Laura Macauley, Nora Meyer, Karl Miller, Blake Morrison, Ellie Ratcliffe, Ryan Roberts, Ahdaf Soueif, Stephen Wall and Patricia Wheatley; and to Stuart Hamilton, whose dedication to preserving his brother's work made this book possible. The Introduction and Notes frequently have recourse to comments made by Ian Hamilton in interview, in particular *Ian Hamilton in Conversation with Dan Jacobson* in the 'Between the Lines' series (London, 2002), which also contains a biographical introduction and an invaluable bibliography. Appendix 2 is especially indebted to a conversation with Peter Dale published in *Agenda*, Volume 31, No. 2: 'Reconsidering the Sixties' (1993), and another, with Gerry Cambridge, in *The Dark Horse*, No. 3 (1996). I also cite various contributions to *Another Round at the Pillars: Essays, Poems and Reflections on Ian Hamilton*, a Festschrift edited by David Harsent (Cornwall: Cargo Press, 1999). I am grateful to the editors and publishers of all these for permission to quote extensively from this material. Both Introduction and Notes, again, frequently cite Ian Hamilton's reviews and essays on other poets and writers, many of the most substantial of which are collected in *A Poetry Chronicle* (London, 1973), *Walking Possession: Essays and Reviews 1968–93* (London, 1994) and *The Trouble With Money* (London, 1998).

POEMS 1961–2001

Memorial

Four weathered gravestones tilt against the wall
Of your Victorian asylum.
Out of bounds, you kneel in the long grass
Deciphering obliterated names:
Old lunatics who died here.

The Storm

Miles off, a storm breaks. It ripples to our room.
You look up into the light so it catches one side
Of your face, your tight mouth, your startled eye.
You turn to me and when I call you come
Over and kneel beside me, wanting me to take
Your head between my hands as if it were
A delicate bowl that the storm might break.
You want me to get between you and the brute thunder.
Settling on your flesh my great hands stir,
Pulse on you and then, wondering how to do it, grip.
The storm rolls through me as your mouth opens.

Pretending Not to Sleep

The waiting rooms are full of 'characters'
Pretending not to sleep.
Your eyes are open
But you're far away
At home, *am Rhein*, with mother and the cats.
Your hair grazes my wrist.
My cold hand surprises you.

The porters yawn against the slot-machines
And watch contentedly; they know I've lost.
The last train
Is simmering outside, and overhead
Steam flowers in the station rafters.
Soft flecks of soot begin to settle
On your suddenly outstretched palms.
Your mouth is dry, excited, going home:

The velvet curtains,
Father dead, the road up to the village,
Your hands tightening in the thick fur
Of your mother's Persian, your dreams
Moving through Belgium now, full of your trip.

Trucks

At four, a line of trucks. Their light
Slops in and spreads across the ceiling,
Gleams, and goes. Aching, you turn back
From the wall and your hands reach out
Over me. They are caught
In the last beam and, pale,
They fly there now. You're taking off, you say,
And won't be back.
                          Your shadows soar.
My hands, they can merely touch down
On your shoulders and wait. Very soon
The trucks will be gone. Bitter, you will turn
Back again. We will join our cold hands together.

The Recruits

'Nothing moves,' you say, and stare across the lawn.
'The sun is everywhere. There will be no breeze.'
Birds line the gutters, and from our window
We see cats file across five gardens
To the shade and stand there, watching the sky.
You cry again: 'They know.'
The dead flies pile up on the window sill.
You shudder as the silence darkens, till
It's perfect night in you. And then you scream.

Windfalls

The windfalls ripen on the lawn,
The flies won't be disturbed.
They doze and glisten,
They wait for the fresh falls
To wipe them out. Like warts,
A pair of them sleep on your wrist.
Disabled, sleek, they have their fill.

Another wind prepares. It will shake apples
For these suicidal flies. It will restore
To lethargy your pale, disfigured hand.

Birthday Poem

Tight in your hands,
Your Empire Exhibition shaving mug.
You keep it now
As a spittoon, its bloated doves,
Its 1938
Stained by the droppings of your blood.
Tonight,
Half-suffocated, cancerous,
Deceived,
You bite against its gilded china mouth
And wait for an attack.

Metaphor

Your shadows blossom now about your bed
Discolouring
The last irritated facts.
Your oriental dressing-gown;
Its golden butterflies, laced to their silken leaves,
Ache from the sudden darkness at your door.
You talk of butterflies, their luxuries, their skills
And their imprisonment.
You say,
'By these analogies we live.'

The sound of water trembles at the lip
Of this glass you are about to smash;
Your curtains flame like corrugated shields
Across these late September fields of snow
That are killing you.

Father, Dying

Your fingers, wisps of blanket hair
Caught in their nails, extend to touch
The bedside roses flaking in the heat.
White petals fall.
                    Trapped on your hand
They darken, cling in sweat, then curl,
Dry out and drop away.
                    Hour after hour
They trickle from the branch. At last
It's clean and, when you touch it, cold.
You lean forward to watch the thorns
Pluck on your skin white pools
That bleed as your fist tightens.
'My hand's in flower,' you say. 'My blood
Excites this petal dross. I'll live.'

Bequest

It is midwinter now and I am warm,
Bedridden, glad to be outlived.
My furniture
Surrounds me. I can reach my books.
And you, night after night
Until 'the end',
Will sit with me.

Between us
There are medicines, this pain
And these unfinished poems I bequeath you.
It must often be like this.
We darken gently as you count the days.
Your breath on mine,
Monotonously warm.

Midwinter

Entranced, you turn again and over there
It is white also. Rectangular white lawns
For miles, white walls between them. Snow.
You close your eyes. The terrible changes.

White movements in one corner of your room.
Between your hands, the flowers of your quilt
Are stormed. Dark shadows smudge
Their faded, impossible colours, but won't settle.

You can hear the ice take hold.
Along the street
The yellowed drifts, cleansed by a minute's fall,
Wait to be fouled again. Your final breath
Is in the air, pure white, and moving fast.

Last Respects

Your breathing slightly disarrays
A single row of petals
As you lean over him. Your fingers,
In the air, above his face,
Are elegant, perplexed. They pause
At his cold mouth
But won't touch down; thin shadows drift
On candle smoke into his hair.
Your friendly touch
Brings down more petals:
A colourful panic.

Funeral

The tall weeds trail their hair
And spiral lazily
Up from their barnacled black roots
As if to touch,
Though hardly caring,
The light that polishes their quiet pool.

Beyond this damp, unpopular beach
The funeral cars,
Bathed in their own light,
Are gliding home now
And the first spray is breaking on my skin.

This tolerant breeze will not disturb us,
Father and son. The hotel is alight.

Epitaph

The scent of old roses and tobacco
Takes me back.
It's almost twenty years
Since I last saw you
And our half-hearted love affair goes on.

You left me this:
A hand, half-open, motionless
On a green counterpane.
Enough to build
A few melancholy poems on.

If I had touched you then
One of us might have survived.

Complaint

I've done what I could. My boys run wild now.
They seek their chances while their mother rots here.
And up the road, the man,
My one man, who touched me everywhere,
Falls to bits under the ground.

I am dumpy, obtuse, old and out of it.
At night, I can feel my hands prowl over me,
Lightly probing at my breasts, my knees,
The folds of my belly,
Now and then pressing and sometimes,
In their hunger, tearing me.
I live alone.

My boys run, leaving their mother as they would a stone
That rolls on in the playground after the bell has gone.
I gather dust and I could almost love the grave.
To have small beasts room in me would be something.
But here, at eight again, I watch the blossoms break
Beyond this gravel yard.
I know how to behave.

Night Walk

Above us now, the bridge,
The dual carriageway,
And the new cars, their solemn music
Cool, expectant, happily pursued.
Tonight, your eyes half-closed, you want to lean
But patiently, upon my arm.

You want to sleep, imagining you see
Again thin-shadowed, anxious pools of light
Swarm quietly across this dark canal
And fade upon the weeds;
These soft horizons,
Softer than my touch.

Poem

Ah, listen now,
Each breath more temperate, more kind,
More close to death.
Sleep on
And listen to these words
Faintly, and with a tentative alarm,
Refuse to waken you.

Admission

The chapped lips of the uniformed night-porter
Mumble horribly against the misted glass
Of our black ambulance.
Our plight
Inspires a single, soldierly, contemptuous stare
And then he waves us on, to Blighty.

Last Waltz

From where we sit, we can just about identify
The faces of these people we don't know:
A shadowed semi-circle
Ranged around the huge, donated television set
That dominates the ward.

The 'Last Waltz' floods over them
Illuminating
Fond, exhausted smiles. And we,
As if we cared, are smiling too.

To each lost soul, at this late hour
A medicated pang of happiness.

Nature

I sit beneath this gleaming wall of rock
And let the breeze lap over me.
It's pleasant
Counting syllables in perfect scenery
Now that you've gone.

Home

This weather won't let up. Above our heads
The houses lean upon each other's backs
And suffer the dark sleet that lashes them
Downhill. One window is alight.

'That's where I live.' My father's sleepless eye
Is burning down on us. The ice
That catches in your hair melts on my tongue.

The Visit

They've let me walk with you
As far as this high wall. The placid smiles
Of our new friends, the old incurables,
Pursue us lovingly.
Their boyish, suntanned heads,
Their ancient arms
Outstretched, belong to you.

Although your head still burns
Your hands remember me.

The Vow

O world leave this alone
At least
This shocked and slightly aromatic fall of leaves
She gathers now and presses to her mouth
And swears on. Swears that love,
What's left of it,
Will sleep now, unappeased, impossible.

Your Cry

Your mouth, a thread of dying grass
Sealed to its lower lip,
At last is opening. We are alone,
You used to say,
And in each other's care.

Your cry
Has interrupted nothing and our hands,
Limp in each other's hair,
Have lost their touch.

Awakening

Your head, so sick, is leaning against mine,
So sensible. You can't remember
Why you're here, nor do you recognize
These helping hands.
My love,
The world encircles us. We're losing ground.

Aftermath

You eat out of my hand,
Exhausted animal. Your hair
Hangs from my wrist.

I promise that when your destruction comes
It will be mine
Who could have come between you.

Words

You've had no life at all
To speak of, silent child.
Tonight
Your mother's German lullaby
Broke into tears
Upon your dreamless head
And you awoke in joy
To welcome her unanswerable cry.

Old Photograph

You are wandering in the deep field
That backs on to the room I used to work in
And from time to time
You look up to see if I am watching you.
To this day
Your arms are full of the wild flowers
You were most in love with.

Neighbours

From the bay windows
Of the mouldering hotel across the road from us
Mysterious, one-night itinerants emerge
On to their balconies
To breathe the cool night air.

We let them stare
In at our quiet lives.
They let us wonder what's become of them.

Breaking Up

He's driving now,
The father of your family,
Somewhere up north. Before he left
You shared out your three hundred books
Together. He has taken those you've read
And left behind
Those you have secretly decided
Are unreadable.

Newscast

The Vietnam war drags on
In one corner of our living-room.
The conversation turns
To take it in.
Our smoking heads
Drift back to us
From the grey fires of South-east Asia.

Curfew

It's midnight
And our silent house is listening
To the last sounds of people going home.
We lie beside our curtained window
Wondering
What makes them do it.

Now and Then

The white walls of the Institution
Overlook a strip of thriving meadowland.
On clear days, we can walk there
And look back upon your 'second home'
From the green shelter
Of this wild, top-heavy tree.

It all seems so long ago. This afternoon
A gentle sun
Smiles on the tidy avenues, the lawns,
The miniature allotments,
On the barred windows of the brand-new
Chronic block, 'our pride and joy'.
At the main gate
Pale visitors are hurrying from cars.

It all seems so far away. This afternoon
The smoke from our abandoned cigarettes
Climbs in a single column to the sky.
A gentle sun
Smiles on the dark, afflicted heads
Of young men who have come to nothing.

Retreat

A minute pulsation of blood-red
Invades one corner of your wounded eye.
You hear it throb
In perfect harmony with our despair
And I'm no comfort to you any more.

Friends

'At one time we wanted nothing more
Than to wake up in each other's arms.'
Old enemy,
You want to live forever
And I don't
Was the last pact we made
On our last afternoon together.

In Dreams

To live like this:
One hand in yours, the other
Murderously cold; one eye
Pretending to watch over you,
The other blind.
                    We live in dreams:
These sentimental afternoons,
These silent vows,
How we would starve without them.

Bedtime Story

From your cautiously parked car
We watch the lights go out
Along this reputable cul-de-sac.

Your garden furniture
Sleeps in a haze of cultivated blossom
And the two trees you have been working on
All summer
Doze beside your garden gate.

'So many families. So many friends.'
In love at last, you can imagine them
Pyjama'd and half-pissed
Extinguishing another perfect day.

Poet

'Light fails; the world sucks on the winter dark
And everywhere
Huge cities are surrendering their ghosts . . .'
The poet, listening for other lives
Like his, begins again: 'And it is all
Folly . . .'

Critique

In Cornwall, from the shelter of your bungalow
You found the sea 'compassionate'
And then 'monotonous',
Though never, in all fairness,
'*Inconnue*'. There was no hiding it.
Your poems wouldn't do.

We sat on for another hour or two,
Old literary pals,
You chewing on your J&B
And me with your dud manuscripts
Face downward on my knee.

'It's been a long time', you said,
'I'll race you to the sea.'

Ghosts

The scrubbed, magnificently decked coffin
Skates, like a new ship, into the fiery deep.
On dry land,
The congregation rustles to its knees.

From my corner pew
I command an unobstructed view
Of your departure.
If you had been lying on your side
I might have caught your unsuspecting eye.

Out on the patio, at dusk,
The floral tributes. I could almost swear
That it was you I saw
Sniffing the wreath-scented air
And counting the bowed heads of your bereaved.

Rose

In the delicately shrouded heart
Of this white rose, a patient eye,
The eye of love,
Knows who I am, and where I've been
Tonight, and what I wish I'd done.

I have been watching this white rose
For hours, imagining
Each tremor of each petal to be like a breath
That silences and soothes.
'Look at it,' I'd say to you
If you were here: 'it is a sign
Of what is brief, and lonely
And in love.'

But you have gone and so I'll call it wise:
A patient breath, an eye, a rose
That opens up too easily, and dies.

Anniversary

You have forgotten almost everything
We promised never to let go.
I even wonder if you know
Why at the dead of night you went with me
To face those blindly drifting gusts of snow,
Why it had to be that route we took
And not the other, why
After all that's gone between us
We still seem to be together.

In this deadeningly harsh weather
It's a waste of breath trying to explain
Over again. You walk ahead
Unsteadily. I let you. A red coat
Disappearing into snow; the green branch
You were carrying abandoned:
Separate lives
Now distantly marooned.
You're small, and smaller still
With every move you make.
In ten seconds we will hear it break.

Returning

It isn't far. Come with me. There's a path
We used to take. There is a stream,
A thin ripple, really, of white stones
Dislodged from a dilapidated boundary
Between two now-forgotten fields;
There is a tree, a muddily abandoned sprawl
Off-balance – the one tall thing
You could see from where I walked with her.

What it all looks like now I wouldn't know,
But come with me. It was an early dusk
On that day too, and just as sickeningly cold,
And when I called to her: 'It isn't far',
She said: 'You go.'
Somewhere ahead of us
I thought I could foresee
A silence, a new path,
A clean sweep of solitude, downhill.

Dear friend, I wish you could have seen
This place when it was at its best,
When I was,
But it isn't far. It isn't far. Come with me.

Remember This

You won't remember this, but I will:
A gradually tightening avenue of trees
And where it locks
What seems from here the most yearningly delicate
Intrusion of white leaves
May yet blacken the unclouded pool of sun
That summons you.
                    Keep going
Even though I mean to stay; keep going
Even though I can't any more imagine
What I'll find most hard to bear
On the way back from here,
On the way home
To where we first vowed we'd try again to say:
You won't remember this.

New Year

You are not with me, and for all I know
You may not have survived.
The weather's 'almost gone'
You used to say
And so it has.
                    Lost child
Look over there: this unprofitable
Three dozen yards of land, still fortified
Against non-residents, has had its day;
The trees you couldn't climb,
Fatigued, are clownishly spiked out
On an expressionless, half-darkened wall of sky.
Home far from home.

So far as I can see, none of it,
Nor of us, my love, minds much what's next to go:
Another lapse of the delighted heart
That's given up on you,
Another pleasantness to wait for, and then wait again,
Then wait; the infant lawns
You weren't supposed to walk on, semi-swamps
Of glitteringly drenched green.

Colours

Yes, I suppose you taught us something.
That bottle-green priest's dressing-gown,
For instance, that they tried to tog you up in
For your last overnight at the Infirmary.
'My Celtic shroud', you called it
And when no one laughed: 'Before morning
Your dear daddy will be Ibrox blue.'

Familiars

If you were to look up now you would see
The moon, the bridge, the ambulance,
The road back into town.
                              The river weeds
You crouch in seem a yard shorter,
A shade more featherishly purple
Than they were this time last year;
The caverns of 'your bridge'
Less brilliantly jet-black than I remember them.

Even from up here, though, I can tell
It's the same unfathomable prayer:
If you were to look up now would you see
Your moon-man swimming through the moonlit air?

Larkinesque

Your solicitor and mine sit side by side
In front of us, in Courtroom Number Three.
It's cut and dried,
They've told us, a sure-fire decree:
No property disputes, no tug-of-love,
No bitching about maintenance. Well done.

All that remains
Is for the Judge to 'wrap it up', and that's how come
We sit here, also side by side
(Although to each of us we are 'the other side'),
And listen to Forbes-Robertson and Smythe,
Our champions, relax.
                              It turns out, natch,
They went to the same school,
That neither of them ever thought
The other had it in him to . . . and yet,
Well, here they were, each peddling
Divorces for a crust. Too bloody true.
And did not each of them remember well
Old Spotty Moses and his 'magic snake',
Mott Harrison's appalling breath, Butch Akenside's
Flamboyant, rather pushy suicide?
Indeed. Where were *they* now? (Aside,
That is to say, from Akenside.) Ah well.

'And you, old man, did you, well, take the plunge?'
No bloody fear: Forbes-Robertson, it seems,
Keeps Labradors, and Smythe keeps his relationships
'Strictly Socratic'. When you'd seen
What they'd seen . . . and so on.

Their rhythms were becoming Larkinesque
And so would mine if I were made to do
This kind of thing more often. As it is,
The morning sun, far from 'unhindered', animates
The hands I used to write about with 'lyric force'.
Your hands
Now clutching a slim volume of dead writs.

The Forties

'The self that has survived those trashy years',
Its 'austere virtue' magically intact. Well then,
He must have asked himself, is this
The 'this is it'; that encapsulable Life
I never thought to find
And didn't seek: beginning at the middle
So that in the end
The damage is outlived by the repair?

At forty-five
I'm father of the house now and at dusk
You'll see me take my 'evening stroll'
Down to the dozing lily pond:
From our rear deck, one hundred and eleven yards.
And there I'll pause, half-sober, without pain
And seem to listen; but no longer 'listen out'.
And at my back,
Eight windows, a veranda, the neat plot
For your (why not?) 'organic greens',
The trellis that needs fixing, that I'll fix.

House Work

How can I keep it steady?
Don't you see
The weakened plank, dead-centre?
And I can't believe that you can fail to hear
This slight but certain tremor underfoot
When you steal in, so lovingly invisible,
To polish my condemned, three-legged desk.

The Garden

This garden's leaning in on us, green-shadowed
Shadowed green, as if to say: be still, don't agitate
For what's been overgrown –
Some cobbled little serpent of a path,
Perhaps, an arbour, a dry pond
That you'd have plans for if this place belonged to you.
The vegetation's rank, I'll grant you that,
The weeds well out of order, shoulder-high
And too complacently deranged. The trees
Ought not to scrape your face, your hands, your hair
Nor so haphazardly swarm upwards to impede
The sunlit air you say you need to breathe
In summertime. It shouldn't be so dark
So early.
       All the same, if I were you,
I'd let it be. Lay down your scythe. Don't fidget
For old clearances, or new. For one more day
Let's listen to our shadows and be glad
That this much light has managed to get through.

Again

That dream again: you stop me at the door
And take my arm, but grievingly.
Behind you, in the parlour, I can see
The bow of a deep sofa, blanketed in grey,
And next to it, as if at harbourside,
A darker grey, rough-sculpted group of three.
Three profiles sombrely inclined,
Long overcoats unbuttoned, hats in hand:
Night-mariners, with eyes of stone,
And yet the eyes seem stricken.
Is it that they too can hardly bear
What's happened? What *has* happened? Who?

At Evening

Arriving early, I catch sight of you
Across the lawn. You're hovering:
A silver teaspoon in one hand
(The garden table almost set)
And in the other, a blue vase.
For the few seconds I stand watching you
It seems half-certain you'll choose wrong
– Well, not exactly wrong, but dottily,
Off-key. You know,
That dreaminess in you we used to smile about
(My pet, my little lavender, my sprite),
It's getting worse.
I'd talk to you about it if I could.

Soliloquy

'We die together though we live apart'
You say, not looking up at me,
Not looking up.
                    'I mean to say,
Even were we actually to die in unison,
Evaporating in each other's arms,
We'd still have ended up – well, wouldn't we? –
Dying for a taste, our first and last,
Of unaloneness:
                    we'd have dreamed,
Dreamed up a day utterly unclouded
By the dread that not quite yet but soon,
Although, please God, not very soon,
We will indeed be whispering
Wretchedly, in unison, your breath on mine:
I might as well be dead,
Or we might. Do you follow? Are you
With me? Do you see?'

Steps

Where do we find ourselves? What is this tale
With no beginning and no end?
We know not the extremes. Perhaps
There are none.
We are on a kind of stair. The world below
Will never be regained; was never there
Perhaps. And yet it seems
We've climbed to where we are
With diligence, as if told long ago
How high the highest rung.
Alas: this lethargy at noon,
This interfered-with air.

Fever

We are dreaming of a shape within a blur:
A hairline thread, a fracture that won't knit,
A flaw that won't be fatal but won't fade.
We are dreaming of old damage, scars
That hold but never heal.
We are dreaming of discolorations,
Tubes the size of pinholes, mucky lungs.

We are dreaming of a dream within a dream:
A seaside sickroom breeze,
The blue curtains that lilt with it,
Floral walls. And in the air,
Anxiety, not ours.
I think we are dreaming of young mothers,
Of iodine, thermometers, cool hands.

Resolve

You used to know. You used to know
My other room, my books,
My altered times of day.
You used to know my friends.

You used to know how hard I tried
And how foolhardily I'd swear
That this time I'd not falter. You could tell
What lay in store for me, and what I'd spent
And what might be retrieved.

Enchantress, know-all, Queen of Numbers, Muse,
You knew all this. And what do you know now?
More of the same, you'll say,
But toothless, blind, forgetful. Well, perhaps.

Unlock my hand,
Let's call this 'for the last time'.
When you go,
Don't murmur, as you used to, 'Yes, I know.'

Dream Song

He called you Master of beauty,
Craftsman of the snowflake, your contrivances
Beyond compare, or competition.
He knew little of your character,
Your background, or your 'motivation'
Famously mysterious and manifold.

Most nights it was enough
To seek to praise, imploringly,
Your work so far, your imminent
Deep-thirsting rose,
For instance, your now dead
And yet triumphant to remember

Daffodil, your giant tree almost afloat
Again outside his window,
Punctual and unthrifty in its green.
Great Lord,
Was it indeed your will
That he should thus so humanly
Heartsore pick up his pen and look the other way?

Responsibilities

Imagining you on your own,
I'm vigilant.
You've heard me, I can tell.
A rustle in the kitchen leaves
Above your head, a semi-stifled click
Somewhere below, an errant chime
An hour or so into your sleeplessness:
Ghost tremors,
They don't keep you company,
Not now, and they won't bring me back,
Not this time. 'Please
Leave me alone,' I've heard you cry
And you have heard me rustle in reply,
Or click, or chime: 'Don't make me go.'

Biography

Who turned the page? When I went out
Last night, his Life was left wide-open,
Half-way through, in lamplight on my desk:
The Middle Years.
Now look at him. Who turned the page?

Family Album

In this one you look miles away
And I'm wearing a tolerant half-smile
That seems to say I've fixed things rather well.
What things?

The turreted edifice behind us
I don't recognize at all. Nor can I place
These avenues of trees, abundant
But municipal, well-kept.

It's evidently summertime, and getting late,
A little before supper-bell, I'd guess,
Or prayers.
Another grainy, used-up afternoon.

But what about that speck
There, to the right, a figure on a bench
Perhaps, not looking and yet looking?
And who does that dark, motionless dog-shape belong to?
There, beside that tree.
And look at how those shadows,
So uneven, seem to corrugate the lawn.
We're out at sea,
So you would say, or would have said.

Not all that many years ago,
I might have asked you to explain
Where, when and who,
And maybe why,
And you'd have wanted to. You'd have been
Able to. Not now, though,
Not today. Don't even try.

Almost Nothing

It is an almost-nothing thing, I know
But it won't let me go. It's not a scent
Exactly, but on hot days or at night I do remember it
As slightly burnt, or over-ripe:
Black wheatfields, sulphur, skin.
It's noiseless too
Although from time to time I think I've heard it
Murmuring: a prayer
Presumably, a promise or a plea. And no,
It's not at all substantial; that's to say
It's substanceless, it's not a thing
That you could touch or see.

It doesn't hurt but it belongs to me.
What do we call it then,
This something in the air, this atmosphere,
This imminence?
Today, because you've turned away,
I'll call it nothing much,
I'll call it, since you're frightened, here to stay.

UNPUBLISHED AND UNCOLLECTED POEMS

Your Place

The main street burns. It's two blocks to your place.
There are girls everywhere and the one I'm looking at
Might. She holds my stare a second, then, compassionate,
She lets it go. And I can hardly see her face
For people. Yet when, like a great slow fish, she turns
Into the tide, baring her teeth at me, I look down
At the hot stone crumbling under my feet, at the brown
Dust there. She moves on. The main street burns.
It's two blocks to your place. There are girls everywhere.

Parting

We sprawl here, friend, and flick the butts around,
Don't talk much and, like failing lovers, stare
At who comes in. But we can't sink our fear
In bed. We reminisce. And when the past
Has broken through to blind us, then recedes,
Look how we grub about for what the beach
Can hold. Our fingers, shot with cramp,
Devoutly pick at what we've been,
Accept the rotten flesh that comes too clean.

Us and Flies

It's cooler now. At last the flies
That stupid with the heat have spun
About my head all day, awake and go.
They leave their dead. And I feel good.

Yet I'd know this of you that stretch
Here at my elbow, you that reach
So hard for life it thrills you down
Your delicate dark sides. What is it,
Now you're there at last, brought low,
That in your head can grow
Such quaint persuasions as you spite
Your broken body with by fighting so?

You flap those ragged wings as if
You didn't know this is the way
Things are between your lot and mine.

You tremble now to poise, then fall
Back on your side. I put you down.
Eagerly, my hand assumes the stain.

Fears

You say that ghosts invade your peace at night
That waking when it's barely light
You shrink to find your curtains fly
Or pale, alert, you catch some sly
Proud move there at your door. You cry
All this at me now. 'Look', I try,
'There's nothing there you couldn't tame
As meek as these rough hands that strain
Above you now. Look. See them. Call their name.'
I touch you to be calm again.
To turn. 'Come, turn', I plead. But no.
And when I move, you say 'No more.
I'll have no more these talons at my thigh.'
Then crane over me, frantic, seeking the light.

Apology

At morning now it is the brush
Of your damp hair along my blood
That wakes me. And your look that kills.
Last night I stared you down so hard
You cried to get away. You couldn't
Breathe. My cold hands made you cry.
And now for shame these bullies would
Mould you to peace again, they speed
Such scares across your skin as I
Had never guessed their postures could
Persuade. You bristle to my touch.
You moan. You move beyond my skills.

The Veteran

A grey, hard-veined old ruin now, he sits
Around the house most days and speaks only
On small affairs. He keeps his schedule tight
And guards his property with bitterness.
I got him talking once. With great contempt
He asked me what I did. I said I wrote
Three times before he got it. Then he leant
So close I took his rotten breath inside me
And asked: 'What about?'; and he is right.

The Silence

You walk ahead of me. The silence stands
On these white fields for miles at either side
And on their frozen lake. The trees
That file beside us can almost touch
Across our path. They are like hands
Troubled by some forgotten prayer:
They are sustained by their burden
Of silence. It is substantial
And stretches between us now. Your words,
Reverberating on it, as the branch you throw
Strikes angrily across the banks of snow
To disappear, are wasted.

The Birds

She saw it from a distance seem to burn
Along the branches of her orchard trees,
Then disappear. All afternoon
She had kept watch. The smaller birds,
Assembled on the bitten lawn
In perfect rows, had waited with her.
Soon, she consoled them, soon.

Their claws stretch and unstretch, deep in the ground.
Between the broken trees, there are avenues
That flutter as she talks and seem to run
To the horizon without moving.

She stalls above all this and seems to see
Black on the whitest hill, the furthest tree.

Vigil

These ancient lamps, diminishing each day,
Will never taste the dark worlds they whimper for.
These wounds,
Though we have nourished them for years,
Will be the freshest of sweet tears
Tomorrow. And the lost will not be found.

Fair

Pink flames of candy floss, rotating stars
On sticks, a healthy coconut,
Two pop-eyed plastic dolls,
A weeping gnome:
In the shadow of the Great Wheel
We count what we have won
And we are 'tired, but happy'.

Untranslatable

'There are certain lines – whole poems, even:
I have no idea what they mean;
It's what I can't grasp that draws me back to them.'
Yours used to be like that, and so did his.

Work in Progress

A six foot three American breathologist
Has cornered me for cocktails; 'Suck on these',
He says, and chucks me a slim vol.
Entitled: *Big*. Two words a line, at most,
Nine lines a page, typography diseased,
It's signed: 'To Ian, in pulse-harmony –
You dig? Love, Irv. November, seventy-three.'
And on the sleeve, a photograph:
Irv felling trees.

An Alternative Agenda

(Not actually spoken by the Convener of a Conference on Literary Journals held at the Australian National University at Canberra.)

We're gathered here today
In Canberra
To discourse on The Literary Journal:
Its role – Now, Then,
Tomorrow afternoon, when (by the way)
We have a change
Of personnel.
Jon Culler has got toothache;
In his stead, (relax, you kiwis),
An unlucky break:
The expat. Peter Porter, with some stuff
You can quite happily ignore
On why he thinks professors are a bore.
Stuff him. We welcome too,
From *Critical Inquiry*, our lone Yank:
W.J.T. Mitchell seems at first
Unsettlingly cheery. Underneath
He's ninety per cent Theory,
One of us. While others idly prate
Tom will 'articulate',
Post-'68.

Which brings us to the ones
We still most love to hate.
Also imported from Abroad
We have three Pom belles-lettrists
Who, to judge from their expressions,
Might not be turning up
To all our sessions:

The *LRB*'s Karl Miller, gargoyle-like,
Seems half-asleep. (The other half
Is threatening to weep.)
And from the *TLS*, Jerry Treglown
Forever savouring some private joke,
And Ian Hamilton,
All-purpose lit. hist. hack,
Invisible behind a cloud of smoke.
This trio you can secretly disdain:
Back numbers
Here to wave the Impo flag
We're here to piss on.

We post-cols
Have actually assembled here
To make it terminally clear
Who runs this culture-site
These days, whose canons
Have dry powder, whose lit-myths
Can stand up to the litmus
Of the newest lit. crit.
The Poms are bloody good
At looking peevish
But wait until we're through
With Grandad Leavis
And big Matt.
That's when we'll see
Who's where it's at.

For four long days
We're planning to attack
These dilettante lib. hums.
On two flanks.
First we will gently Oz them
Into critical narcosis

With deep-stir talk
Of *Quandrant* and of *Scripsi*,
Get them tipsy,
And then, before the bastards can say
'Dingo'
Or even 'symbiosis',
We'll poison them
With our post-modern lingo!

The end – on Day Four – ought to be
Bloodless and undramatic,
Just like me.
Already at death's door,
The Brits will only need
A little more:
For each there'll be one final squirm
As we dispense what is to him
The deadliest life-denying term.
P. Porter, as I see it,
Will be felled by 'phallocratic',
And 'counter-public' should take care
Of Miller. For Treglown
'Matrix' should prove the killer.
If, by some mal-chance, these beauts
Don't *terre* the Poms,
Why then
We'll let them try for size
'NARRATIVIZE'.
Thus, comrades, I envisage
Our old enemies' linguistic long goodbyes.

So guys (both he and she),
Let's to it. Paper One
Today, a neo-radical critique
Of Eagleton's most recent . . .

(By the way,
For Hamilton, who planned to write this up
It seems we'll need no poisoned cup
Of language. The smoke clears.
He is already good and dead:
An old-style bourgeois bullet
Through his old-style rhymer's head.)

Spring

Ahead, a prospect of wild flowers,
Anemones, speedwells,
Those purple ones I still can't put a name to,
Willowherb, deadnettle.
Overhead, an arch of glistening new leaves.
It's Spring and I am sick at heart
Again, but not because of her.
Let's call it a Spring-malady,
A seasonal distress,
A ripe bud that can't remember what comes next.

Negatives

Unorphaned animal,
Imagine this: an afternoon
Not wondering
What happens next, a night
Uninterrupted, a new day
Not necessarily not ours.

Ties

You are harvesting dead leaves again
But don't look up.
The trees aren't your trees now
And anyway, white storm birds sing no song.
Inside the house
He's playing genealogies again,
The usual curse:
His, yours, theirs, everyone's. And hers.

Prayer

Look sir, my hands are steady now,
My brain a cloudless day.
Is that the sound of breakfast down below?
To eat again seems possible.
To breathe?
No problem, Lord, I promise. I'm OK.

Notes

page 3 'Memorial': First published in the *New Statesman*, June 1968.

4 'The Storm': First published in the *London Magazine*, May 1962. There, and in *Universities' Poetry 5*, May 1963 (as 'Storm', under 'R.I. Hamilton') and subsequent printings until *Fifty Poems*, line 9 read 'But settling on your flesh . . .' When Peter Dale's volume of poems *The Storms* was published in 1968, I.H. told him that until then he had himself been considering this same title for the collection he was preparing.

5 'Pretending Not to Sleep': First published in the *New Statesman*, May 1964. (Also the title of I.H.'s first booklet of poems, published later that year.) 'The "characters" referred to in the first line are derelicts who have cultivated the knack of sleeping in sitting positions, so as not to be moved on': I.H., Poetry Book Society Bulletin, Summer 1970. Line 5, '*Am Rhein*': [at] by the Rhine. Line 19, 'Your mother's Persian': a coat made from the black, tightly curled fur of Persian lambs. I.H. married the German-born Gisela Dietzel in 1963.

6 'Trucks': First published in the *Observer*, January 1963, in a slightly longer version with different lineation:

> At four, a line of trucks. Their light
> Slops in and spreads across the ceiling,
> Gleams and goes. Aching, you turn
> Back from the wall and your hands
> Reach out over me. They are caught
> In the last beam and, pale, they fly
> There now. Laughing, you nudge me to look.
> You're taking off, you say, and won't be back.
>
> Your shadows soar. My hands, they can merely touch
> Down on your shoulders and wait. Very soon
> The trucks will be gone. Bitter, you will turn
> Back again. We will join our cold hands together.

Line 3, 'Gleams, and goes': cf. 'Dover Beach' by Matthew Arnold: '. . . on the French coast the light / Gleams and is gone'. Arnold's poem was an important one for Hamilton. See also 'Fears', p.72, and 'Apology', p.73.

7 'The Recruits': Pared down for *Fifty Poems* from the version first published in *Universities' Poetry 4*, April 1962, then in the *Observer*, May
1962, *Pretending Not to Sleep* and *The Visit*:

> 'Nothing moves,' you say, and stare across the lawn
> At the trees, loafing in queues, their leaves rigid;
> At the flowers, edgy, poised. You turn and cry:
> 'The sun is everywhere. There will be no breeze.'
>
> Birds line the gutters, and from our window
> We see cats file across five gardens
> To the shade and stand there, tense and sullen,
> Watching the sky. You cry again: 'They know.'
>
> The dead flies pile up on the window sill.
> You scoop them into heaps. You weep on them.
> You shudder as the silence darkens, till
> It's perfect night in you. And then you scream.

The version in John Fuller's cyclostyled typescript (see 'Note on the
Text') has an isolated final (thirteenth) line: 'And my damp flesh
crawls. This is the day.' Peter Dale comments: 'This poem was written
at the height of the Cold War, in the months preceding the Cuban
Missile Crisis' (a stand-off between the US and Soviet governments
about the deployment of Russian nuclear missiles in Cuba, that
brought the two super-powers to the brink of war in October 1962).
'Ian, I remember, was marginally connected to the Committee of 100
who used to do sit-down protests. The cats did exactly what he said
crossing the long garden of 99 [Woodstock Road, Oxford, where both
I.H. and Dale had rooms for a time]. Gisela [I.H.'s first wife] had this
incredible empathy for living creatures. Hence, presumably, those
flies – in other early poems, too.' (See 'Us and Flies', p.71, and 'Windfalls', p.8.) In the chapter on Robert Lowell in *Against Oblivion*, I.H.
writes 'In his 1963 volume [*For the Union Dead*] . . . Lowell's so-called
"confessional" intimacy of address makes itself hospitable to public
themes: in particular, the threat of nuclear extinction – a vividly felt
probability at that time'.

8 'Windfalls': This was pruned back in successive stages from the
thirteen-line original published in the Christmas 1962 Poetry Supplement of the Poetry Book Society (edited by John Fuller), to the
slightly shorter versions that appeared in *Pretending Not to Sleep*,
Poetry Introduction 1 and *The Visit*, finally to the four lines in *Fifty
Poems*:

> The windfalls ripen on the lawn,
> The flies won't be disturbed.
> They doze and glisten;
> They wait for the fresh falls to wipe them out.

When he interviewed I.H. for his magazine *Dark Horse* (1996), Gerry Cambridge asked about the cutting of 'Windfalls'. I.H. commented: 'I just wanted to get rid of bad things in it ... I was in rather a strict mood that day, and they were re-issuing this poem, so I thought I could get rid of the worst bits. I struck them out – a man of integrity – only to find I'd made it even worse.' The version from *The Visit* is printed on p.8, in accordance with these remarks and because the 'pale, disfigured hand' and its lethargy so clearly belong with the other sickly hands, the claustrophobia and *malaise* of I.H.'s poems of this period. (Compare, too, the flies in 'Us and Flies', p.71, and 'The Recruits', p.7.) It should be noted however that the four-line version was retained for *Sixty Poems*, so I.H. either forgot or changed his mind about having 'made it even worse'.

9 'Birthday Poem': First published in *Agenda*, 3/5, September 1964, in two stanzas, separated after line 6. There, as in *Pretending Not to Sleep*, *Poetry Introduction 1* and *The Visit*, there were no commas after 'doves', 'Tonight' and 'Deceived'. 'The Empire Exhibition occurred in 1938, the year in which the speaker in the poem had been born': I.H. (b.1938), Poetry Book Society Bulletin, Summer 1970. I.H. was the second son of Robert Tough Hamilton and Daisy, *née* McKay; his father was from Glasgow, 'Second City of the Empire'. (In 1936 they moved to King's Lynn, where I.H. was born, and in 1951 the family moved to Darlington, where Hamilton senior died shortly after- wards.) Held in Glasgow's Bellahouston Park from May to December 1938, the Exhibition was an attempt to boost Glasgow's economy, recovering from the Depression of the 1930s. It was opened by King George VI and Queen Elizabeth and attracted 12 million visitors to its purpose-built pavilions.

10 'Metaphor': First published in *Pretending Not to Sleep* where line 10, 'By these analogies we live', was followed by the line 'And smile in agony'. This line was dropped for *The Visit* and each succeeding vol- ume. In an I.H. typescript the poem also has an epigraph from Aris- totle which was dropped from all published versions: 'But the greatest thing by far is to have a command of metaphor. This alone cannot be imparted by another'. Line 14, 'these late September fields of snow': see 'Father, Dying', p.11, and 'Midwinter', p.13, and notes below.

11 'Father, Dying': First published in *Paris Review* 29, Winter/Spring
    1963, and in *Universities' Poetry* 5, May 1963 (under 'R.I. Hamilton').
    In the latter it had a second section of ten lines, in two stanzas:

> II
>
> Entranced, you turn again and over there
> It is white also. Rectangular white lawns
> For miles, white walls between them. Snow.
> You close your eyes. The terrible changes.
>
> White movements in one corner of your room.
> Between your hands, the flowers of your quilt
> Are stormed. Dark shadows smudge
> Their faded, impossible colours
> But do not settle. At your head,
> Banked up, white as the snow, fat pillows.

To line 9, 'But do not settle', this is identical to the opening stanzas of
'Last Illness' (later 'Midwinter', see p.13 and note), first published
three months earlier; though the two-part 'Father, Dying' could have
been accepted for publication before that. In both these early versions, the thirteen lines retained as 'Father, Dying' had no paragraph
spacings and the thorns (lines 9/10) 'print on your skin' etc. Slight
variations to the final three lines occur in the versions published in
Poetry Introduction 1 and *The Visit*:

> That bleed as your fist tightens. 'My hand's
> In flower', you say. 'My blood excites
> This petal dross. I'll live.'

Cf. Percy Bysshe Shelley, 'Ode to the West Wind': 'I fall upon the thorns
of life! I bleed!' The white petals, thorns, etc., have more than a sugges-
tion of 'the Nineties' about them, and even a vestigial hint, via the
Nineties, of Mallarmé and the Symbolists (see also 'Rose', p.43). An I.H.
holograph of the poem has the title 'Petals', and a typewritten draft
fragment of another, unfinished I.H. poem from the 1960s begins,

> You called them day-lilies and sure enough
> They were dead by morning. You lay awake
> For hours, imagining that in the dark
> There must be rain, of these orange petals,
> Falling, and that you would sleep better
> Once you had tasted it . . .

(As with other drafts of this period – see the notes to 'Funeral' and

'Your Cry' – 'you' could conceivably refer to a dying father or a sick wife.) I.H.'s poetic aims at this time were also indebted to the poetry and the precepts of Ezra Pound in his Imagist and *Cathay* phases; cf. Pound's 'In a Station of the Metro':

> The apparition of these faces in the crowd:
> Petals on a wet, black bough

(and see the 'oriental dressing gown' etc. of 'Metaphor', p.10). But of greater importance, perhaps, to this particular poem than Shelley, Symbolism or Pound was 'Gold Mohar', by Bernard Gutteridge (1916–85), which I.H. included in his anthology *The Poetry of War 1939–45*, 1965, and almost certainly knew before that (his essay 'The Forties' was first published in instalments in the *London Magazine* in 1964):

> You dead, my friends, still stay
> Like this exquisite tree
> My eyes must leave, heraldic
> Flowering I will not see
> Scald in April with crimson
> Showers of petals . . .

In 'The Forties' I.H. cites one of Gutteridge's 'industriously modish' similes: 'blood/ Flecking like shredded petals of geranium.' Cf. 'Last Respects', p.14. There could be an echo from another poem by Gutteridge, also included in *The Poetry of War*, in 'Midwinter' (originally 'Last Illness': see p.13 and note below). Robert Tough Hamilton died at the age of fifty-one in 1951, when I.H. was thirteen. 'I hadn't seen him,' I.H. said in his interview with Dan Jacobson; 'well, I'd barely seen him during my childhood, so I felt privileged to have this kind of access . . . It was known that he was going to die. Mother knew. And I think my elder brother knew. So they were comforting each other. But there was nobody to . . . During his last months I used to – not nurse him exactly – but sit around with him . . . My father was in his room and I would drift in there . . . I used to sit there as an errand-boy and got very involved in his predicament . . . I didn't know how ill he was though I'd overheard snatches of people's talk and picked up the general atmosphere, but nobody ever told me he was going to die . . . Then, eventually, he was carted off to hospital . . . And that was upsetting, you know, for a thirteen-year-old lad, and then it became much more upsetting in my twenties when I began to think more about him and what kind of life he had had, what kind of person he was. You lose the pattern, losing a parent when you're young. I also felt the wish to speak to him or in some way to have a relationship with him. And I think that those poems probably come from an impulse of that sort, from the delayed pain or loss.' I.H.'s original title for his first volume of poems when it was accepted for publication by Faber & Faber was 'Father and Son'. (See the Introduction; also the note to 'Colours', p.48.)

12 'Bequest': First published in the *New Statesman*, December 1966, where, as in *Poetry Introduction 1* and *The Visit*, the last three lines formed a separate stanza. 'A dramatic monologue spoken by the father who is addressed in [other] poems': I.H., Poetry Book Society Bulletin, Summer 1970. A typewritten draft of this poem bears the title 'He Always Wanted to Write'.

13 'Midwinter': First published in *The Review*, no. 5, February 1963, then in *Pretending Not to Sleep* and *The Visit*, as 'Last Illness', with these differences in lineation and phrasing after line 7:

> Their faded, impossible colours
> But do not settle.
>
> You hear the ice take hold. Along the street

etc. In *Universities' Poetry 5*, May 1963, the first two stanzas formed a second section of 'Father, Dying' (see p.11 and note). Cf. 'Shillong', by Bernard Gutteridge, which I.H. included in *The Poetry of War 1939–45*, and which has this concluding stanza:

> Testing north towards Tibet the cold
> Austere horizon of coarse green pines
> Holds trapped the waterfall. The wide sky throws
> White clouds towards the annihilating snows.

14 'Last Respects': Between its first publication in *Pretending Not to Sleep* and its reappearance in *The Visit*, this poem lost more than half its original length. The first published version is much more explicit:

> Your breathing slightly disarrays
> A single row of petals
> As you lean over him. Your fingers,
> In the air, above his face,
> Are elegant, perplexed. They pause
> At his cold mouth
> But won't touch down; thin shadows drift
> On candle smoke into his hair.

'It is impossible', you say,
'To be lavishly kind. Exhaustion,
The sedentary life, so many years
Of harrowed continence,
Finished him long before. We never talked.'

Our sympathy distends the candle flames
And ripples pools of light
Across the white tiled walls,
The gladiatorial blooms that colour them
In marble reds and greens, across our hands
In dancing spots of shadow, like a plague;
Our hands, staked out with callow expertise
On the black silk of your ravishing funeral costume.
You say he bored you, that you're glad he's dead.
Your friendly touch brings down more petals
A colourful panic.

An even earlier (typescript) version was more explicit still; line 12 reads 'Of harrowed continence, his vivid rages'. Cf. 'Father, Dying', p.11 and note, and 'Rose', p.43.

15 'Funeral': First published in the *Times Literary Supplement*, July 1964, then (as 'The Funeral') in *Pretending Not to Sleep*; in these and in *The Visit* lines 5 and 9 are bracketed. Both 'Funeral' and 'Nature' ['Absence'] (p.22) derive or partly derive from draft poems which, though quite different, are both called 'Scenery'. In 1963 I.H. sent John Fuller the following version in typescript:

I sit beneath a gleaming wall of rock,
This tolerant breeze hangs on the air
Like the smell of cooking.
The tall weeds trail their hair
And spiral lazily
Up from their barnacled black roots
As if to touch
(Though hardly caring)
The light that polishes their quiet pool.
I keep thinking of the past.

This was never published, though most of it survives in 'Funeral'. Another version of 'Scenery' exists in several typewritten drafts, culminating in this one:

> I sit beneath a gleaming wall of rock.
> This delicate breeze hangs on the air
> Like the smell of cooking. The leaves
> Glint at me as your vivid eyes would
> And this stone under my hand is cold
> As your mouth was when you left me.
> I keep thinking of the past. The mountain shrubs
> Seem to advance upon the empty road. The river
> Laps on white cobbles. Your last smile?
> It's pleasant, counting syllables
> In perfect scenery, now that you're gone.

This too remained unpublished; only the first and last two lines survived, in 'Nature'. As with 'Your Cry' (p.26 and note), key lines and phrases appear at different times to evoke the situation both of the bereaved son and of the helpless lover/carer.

16 'Epitaph': First published in the Poetry Supplement of the Poetry Book Society, Christmas 1969.

17 'Complaint': 'A Mother's Complaint', as published in *Universities' Poetry 4*, April 1962, then in the *London Magazine*, May 1962, was a single stanza of fourteen more-or-less-hexameters. The first eight lines of this became the first twelve of the finished 'Complaint' – the unique instance of a Hamilton poem appearing to get *longer* between published versions; though in fact the changes were to lineation only, and the wording is almost identical:

> I have done what I could. My boys run wild now. They seek
> Their chances while their mother rots here. And up the road
> The man, my one man, who touched me everywhere, falls
> To bits under the ground. I am dumpy, obtuse, old
> And out of it. At night, I can feel my hands prowl
> Over me, lightly probing at my breasts, my knees, the folds
> Of my belly, now and then pressing, and sometimes
> In their hunger, tearing me. I live alone.
> My boys run, leaving their mother as they would a stone
> That rolls on in the playground after the bell has gone.
> I gather dust and I could almost love the grave;
> To have small beasts room in me would be something.
> But here, at eight again, I watch the spider swing
> Over the dirty crocks. I know how to behave.

As printed on p.17, the poem appeared in *Pretending Not to Sleep* and all I.H.'s volumes thereafter. Peter Dale recalls, 'Ian said it was based on his mother – he meant her situation was the trigger for the general idea – which makes the "room" image more potent as she had had to keep paying guests to support the family.' At a poetry reading in 1988 I.H. prefaced 'Complaint' by saying he had based it on a poem by François Villon, the great medieval French poet who was imprisoned for theft and murder. (See 'The Lament of the Fair Armouress at Having Grown Old', in e.g. the Bantam Classics *Complete Works of François Villon*, French originals with facing translations, with an introduction by William Carlos Williams, 1960; also Robert Lowell's version in *Imitations*, 1961.) There are no other known instances of I.H. having acknowledged a French model or source (but see the note to 'Father, Dying', p.92).

18   'Night Walk': First published in the *Times Literary Supplement*, July 1965. Line 3, 'their solemn music' could be a memory of the title of a poem by John Milton: 'At a Solemn Musick'.

19   'Poem': First published in *Pretending Not to Sleep* where, as in *Poetry Introduction 1* it appeared with the dedication 'To G' (Gisela [Dietzel], I.H.'s first wife); and there were no commas after lines 1 and 2.

20   'Admission': First published in the *New Statesman*, December 1968. I.H. worked briefly as a night porter at the Radcliffe Infirmary, Oxford, during one university vacation. Line 6, 'Blighty': military slang for England or the homeland, it came into popular use during the First World War, but was well known to soldiers who had served in India long before. From the Urdu, *Vilayati* or *Bilati*, adj. meaning provincial, removed at some distance: hence adopted by the military for England (*Brewer's Dictionary of Phrase and Fable*).

21   'Last Waltz': First published in the *Listener*, July 1968. The title is that of a pop song – a No. 1 hit for Engelbert Humperdinck in August 1967, and 'ubiquitous at the time of writing': I.H., Poetry Book Society Bulletin, Summer 1970.

22   'Nature': First published in the *New Statesman*, June 1968 (then as 'Absence' in *Poetry Introduction 1*; 'Nature' again thereafter). In these and in *The Visit*, the last line read 'Now that you're gone'. See note to 'Funeral', p.95.

23   'Home': First published in the *New Statesman*, June 1968, as an unbroken eight-line poem in which the sentence 'That's where I live'

had a line to itself; in *The Visit*, the same sentence completes a first, five-line stanza.

24 'The Visit': First published (with slight differences in punctuation) in the *Observer*, November 1967, also in *Poetry Introduction 1*, as 'Visit'; it was 'The Visit' in the volume of that name and thereafter. *The Visit* was also the title of a one-act play by Alun Lewis (see Introduction, and notes to 'In Dreams', p.100, and 'The Veteran', p.109). Line 8, 'Although your head still burns': see 'Awakening', p.27, and note. In a draft titled 'At Least', the poem continued with the seven lines that became the whole of 'Vow' (later 'The Vow': see p.25, and note below). In his interview with Dan Jacobson, asked about 'the connection between the brevity and concentration of the poems and their preoc-cupation with pain', I.H. commented: '. . . Some of those poems are longer poems broken into two because they weren't well glued together; there was nothing to join them properly together. It wasn't a strategy, brevity, if you like, just a technical – ' [D.J.] '*A technical device?*' – 'How much you could get into a short space . . . the whole idea of the power of compression . . . It was more a sense of emotion-al pressure, a claustrophobia, that I wanted to convey. I suppose I could only – in life – sustain that for a short time. And I turned it to my advantage in my verse or tried to. I did try longer pieces but they didn't seem to work.'

25 'The Vow': As 'Vow', first published (with 'Visit') in the *Observer*, November 1967, where, as in *Poetry Introduction 1* and *The Visit*, there were no commas after lines 5 and 6. This was coupled, in the draft-poem 'At Least', with the lines that became 'Visit' (see p.24, and note above). In the late 1950s I.H. was impressed by Anthony Hecht's poem 'The Vow', which, in five regularly-rhymed eight-line stanzas, mourns and commemorates a miscarried child.

26 'Your Cry': First published in PEN *New Poems 1967* as 'After All'. Cf. 'Your Words', an I.H. typescript with autograph emendations:

> Your broken mouth,
> A thread of golden lint
> Sealed to its lower lip,
> Is opening.
> Again
> I watch your pale infected tongue
> Tumble against your teeth
> And slacken there
> And lie.

> What would you say?
> At last
> That this is all:
> Your knuckles gleam upon my wrist
> Imprisoning your dream,
> Articulate.

This was never published. Though the opening lines, revised, became the opening lines of the present poem, 'Your Words' is more than a draft; it is, in fact, a different poem. Its subject could be someone coming round from ECT (see note to 'Awakening', below); but could equally well be the dying father. 'Your Cry' clearly belongs with the poems of love damaged or compromised by mental illness, where the cry is one of female anguish (see Introduction).

27 'Awakening': First published in the *New Statesman*, June 1968. 'One of several poems set in a mental hospital. The woman addressed here is awakening after ECT [electro-convulsive therapy], which impairs the memory': I.H., Poetry Book Society Bulletin, Summer 1970.

28 'Aftermath': First published in the *New Statesman*, June 1968, as an unbroken six-line poem, it appeared as here in *Poetry Introduction 1* and thereafter.

29 'Words': First published in the *London Magazine*, April 1969. 'In this poem the speaker addresses his newly-born child': I.H., Poetry Book Society Bulletin, Summer 1970. 'Her unanswerable cry': cf. 'Your Cry', p.26. 'Your mother's German lullaby': see 'Pretending Not to Sleep', p.5, and note.

30 'Old Photograph': First published in the *London Magazine*, April 1969.

31 'Neighbours': First published in the *New Statesman*, December 1968.

32 'Breaking Up': First published in the *New Statesman*, May 1969.

33 'Newscast': First published in the *London Magazine*, April 1969. Line 1, 'The Vietnam war drags on', etc: beginning as a civil war soon after the division of the country in 1954 and escalating into a major conflict in which the United States was deeply involved, the Vietnam war did not end until 1975. It was one of the first conflicts to be extensively reported on television news broadcasts, and the shocking images seen in millions of American and British homes helped to swell a wave of anti-war public opinion. Recalling the period in an interview

with Gregory LeStage that appeared in *Poetry Review* (Winter 1997), I.H. said: 'The gulf between the idea of poetry as intensely personal and the idea of poetry as a political instrument had become vast. Political poetry had been taken over by the Liverpool Poets or Pop poets or Beat poets ... the people who wrote sloganeering verse about Vietnam and other hot issues. That wasn't the kind of thing we did. If we were to write about Vietnam, it would have to do with going into some field and picking a flower that would somehow faintly remind us of a look or a gesture that distantly might hint of a war in Southeast Asia. But the poem would be about walking in the field.' Effectively satirising his own manner, I.H.'s remarks should not be taken as a final judgement on his poem.

34 'Curfew': First published in the *New Statesman*, December 1968.

35 'Now and Then': First published in the *New Statesman*, April 1969.

36 'Retreat': First published in *Agenda*, 9: 2/3, Spring/Summer 1971 .

37 'Friends': First published in the Poetry Supplement of the Poetry Book Society, Christmas 1970. In several drafts with the title 'Resolution', it is clearer that the (by implication) female speaker of the opening lines is referring to a past love, and that she, her present interlocutor and her previous lover or husband are or have been in a triangular relationship. One of these drafts includes the line 'From your cautiously parked car' which resurfaces in 'Bedtime Story' (p.39).

38 'In Dreams': First published in the *New Statesman*, November 1970. 'In dreams begin responsibility (*OLD PLAY*)' was the epigraph to *Responsibilities*, a volume of poems by W. B. Yeats, published in 1914; 'In Dreams Begin Responsibilities', a short story by the American writer Delmore Schwartz (1913-1966), gave its title to a collection of Schwartz's stories and poems published in 1938. (Schwartz was a contemporary and friend of both Robert Lowell and John Berryman; Lowell's poem 'To Delmore Schwartz' appears in *Life Studies*, and Berryman devotes a sequence in the *Dream Songs*, 146–157, to elegies for 'the Brooklyn poet' who died 'miserably & alone / in New York': see note to 'Dream Song', below.) 'Dreams and Responsibilities' was the title of a review-essay by Colin Falck on A. Alvarez's anthology, *The New Poetry*, in the second number of *The Review*, June/July 1962. In his interview with Dan Jacobson I.H. called the essay 'the nearest thing we [i.e. he as editor, and the poets gathered around the magazine] had to a manifesto'. The opposition was an important one to

I.H.: in his own essay 'The Forties' (1964), for example, discussing the poetry of the Second World War and especially that of Keith Douglas, Alun Lewis and Roy Fuller, he writes, '. . . At worst, the antitheses are too spectacular and the poem will often fade off into cosy nostalgia, a trim domesticated version of Eternal Peace, but at best there is a genuine conflict between the active and the nostalgic, the responsibility and the dream. This kind of conflict is at the centre of the best modern poetry . . .' And in the long biographical introduction he wrote for *Alun Lewis: Selected Poetry and Prose* (1966) it becomes the key to Lewis's personality and writing, from his childhood onwards: 'If Cwmaman [the village in Wales where Lewis grew up] was the source of Lewis's responsibility, then Penbryn [where the family enjoyed summer holidays] encouraged the dream that recurs time and again in his poetry, of isolation in a benevolent, undemanding nature.' See also, the shorter pieces reprinted in *A Poetry Chronicle*, e.g. 'Louis MacNeice' (1963) and 'John Berryman' (1965), *passim*; 'Responsibilities', p.62; and the Introduction.

39 'Bedtime Story': First published in the *New Statesman*, October 1970. See 'Friends', p.37, and note.

40 'Poet': First published in *Returning* where it read, after line 6, 'Folly': 'At this time of night / Even the dogs don't give a shit . . .' A typewritten draft of this poem bears the title 'Styles of Despair': this was the title of the chapter on Cyril Connolly and *Horizon* in I.H.'s *The Little Magazines: A Study of Six Editors* (1976). In it I.H. cites one of Connolly's wartime editorials: 'Yet we must remember that the life many of us are now leading is inimical to the appreciation of literature . . . It is as unfair to judge art in these philistine conditions as if we were seasick', and comments, 'This plangently valetudinarian note was to become a regular feature of *Horizon* and was perhaps its truest, most consistent voice . . .' Connolly is quoted again at the end of the magazine's life: 'A decade of our lives is quite enough to devote to a lost cause such as the pursuit and marketing of quality in contemporary writing.' *The Review*, edited by I.H., had run for ten years from 1962 to '72; *The New Review*, begun in 1974, was to last only four years. (See also I.H.'s later review-essay, 'Poor Cyril'.) Cf. the closing lines of 'This Last Pain', by William Empson:

> Imagine, then, by miracle, with me
> (Ambiguous gifts, as what gods give must be)
>   What could not possibly be there,
>   And learn a style from a despair.

41 'Critique': First published in the *Observer*, May 1972. There and in *Returning* the French adjective *inconnue* ('unknown') was given the incorrect masculine form; 'your J&B' (a brand of whisky) was 'your straw' and the dud manuscripts rested simply 'Upon my knee'. Cf. the 'slim volume of dud writs' in the first published version of 'Larkinesque' (p.50 and note).

42 'Ghosts': First published in the *London Magazine*, June/July 1971.

43 'Rose': First published in the *Times Literary Supplement*, August 1972, with very slight differences in punctuation. 'The Rose' by Theodore Roethke, a longish poem in four sections that has nothing in common with this one beyond the title and its central symbol, was published in *Agenda*, Vol.3 No.4, April 1964; I.H.'s essay on Roethke appeared immediately after it in the same number. (See the note to 'Father, Dying', above.)

44 'Anniversary': First published by the Poem of the Month Club in 1971, then in *The Review*, 29/30, Spring-Summer 1972 (the last issue of the magazine), as 'Remembrance'. See 'The Silence' (p.75) and note; and 'Vigil' (p.77) and note.

45 'Returning': First published in the *Times Literary Supplement*, July 1975; the title poem of the booklet published in 1976. In the booklet, there were slight differences in lineation and phrasing to the central stanza:

> What it all looks like now I wouldn't know,
> But come with me. It was an early dusk
> On that day too, and just as sickeningly cold,
> And when I called to her: 'It isn't far',
> She said: 'You go'. Somewhere ahead of us
> I thought I could foresee
> A silence, a new path,
> A green sweep of solitude
> Downhill.

In the original *TLS* version the lineation was as above and the 'green sweep' (line 16) was 'A blindingly green sweep' (cf. the 'glitteringly drenched green' of 'New Year', p.47). The final version more inspiritingly makes 'a clean sweep' of the image.

46 'Remember This': First published in the *Times Literary Supplement*, December 1976, this was the final poem in *Returning*, which also appeared that month, intended for private distribution.

47 'New Year': First published in the *Times Literary Supplement*, May 1978, where there were commas after lines 3 and 6, the trees (line 9), 'Fatigued, seem[ed] clownishly spiked out / Against an expressionless . . .' etc. and 'the infant lawns' (line 19) were simply 'the lawns'. See note to 'Returning', above.

48 'Colours': First published in the *London Review of Books*, February 1984. Line 5, 'My Celtic shroud': a length of fabric presented to members of some Celtic tribes on acceding to manhood. It served as blanket, cloak and small tent as need demanded, and, at a man's death, was often used as his burial shroud. Line 7, '[Ibrox] blue': the colours of Glasgow Rangers (Ibrox their home ground); their Glasgow rivals Celtic play in green and white hoops. I.H.'s father was originally from Glasgow, and in his interview with Dan Jacobson, I.H. recalled the circumstances of his death: 'There were lots of grins, sick death-jokes, all that . . . Then, eventually, he was carted off to hospital, which is what that Celtic-Rangers poem was about, the final joke he made. He said he'd turn blue – the Rangers team colour – by the morning. Which in fact he did; he didn't last out the night.' (See note to 'Father, Dying', above.)

49 'Familiars': First published in the *London Review of Books*, February 1984.

50 'Larkinesque': First published in the *London Review of Books*, March 1987, where 'animates' (line 33) read 'falls upon' and 'dead' writs (line 36) were 'dud' writs. I.H. wrote appreciatively and even admiringly about the poetry of Philip Larkin (1922–85), from his review of *The Whitsun Weddings*, 1964, to the chapter on Larkin in the posthumously published *Against Oblivion* (2002). I.H. and his first wife were divorced in 1978. Larkin himself never married.
Line 32, 'The morning sun, far from "unhindered"': Larkin makes frequent and effective use of the negative prefix throughout his work, and one of the most celebrated of these is 'a strong / Unhindered moon' in 'Dockery and Son', in *The Whitsun Weddings*. Peter Dale comments: 'In 1964 I wrote a poem, "Eighth Period", which contains the phrase "Unhindered sunset". Larkin's poem was published some time that year. I'm pretty sure I wrote "Eighth Period" before I had read it, but I did later review *The Whitsun Weddings* so I can't be certain. I was living in Newport near Hull at the time and travelled along the same railway as Larkin. Was the parallel use of the epithet a coincidence of our observing similar effects of light or was there a reminiscence? Many years later Ian published "Larkinesque", with the line

"The morning sun . . . [etc]" ; his title and the use of quotation marks
would seem to indicate that he is simply citing Larkin. But Larkin's
moon has become my sun and my sunset, Ian's morning. My poem
was in *The Storms*, 1968, a book dedicated to Ian. So is it coincidence,
citation, influence, unconscious reminiscence? Who can unravel the
mysteries of creativity?' (See, also, 'Dream Song', p.61, line 15:
'Punctual and unthrifty in its green'; and 'Negatives', p.86.) Line 11,
'Forbes Robertson': Sir Johnston Forbes Robertson (1853–1937) was
a celebrated actor and theatre-manager. The name seems, though,
to have been chosen purely for its class associations and musical
properties.

52 'The Forties': First published in the *London Review of Books*, February
1984. The opening lines quote from *Memoirs of Hecate County* (1946),
by Edmund Wilson (1895-1972): 'It had the dignity, that rude yet snug
little house, of everything in my life that was good . . . I could rejoin
my old solitary self, the self for which I really lived and which kept up
its austere virtue, the self which had survived through these trashy
years'. I.H. cites the passage in his review (for the *Sunday Times*) of
The Forties, a volume of Wilson's journals. The review begins, 'In
1940, Edmund Wilson became 45 and thus, as he saw it, definitively
"middle-aged". In that same year, his friend Scott Fitzgerald died –
from an excess of youthfulness, some believed . . . The time had surely
come for some kind of personal consolation, a grateful counting of
the days'. Its almost-last words are 'After two decades of grappling
with the zeitgeist Wilson had every right to start cultivating his own
backyard . . .' I.H. also reviewed Wilson's *The Fifties* (for the *Washing-
ton Post*) and in his preface to *Fifty Poems* he quotes Wilson again, in
relation to 'these poems of my early middle-age': 'I'm not sure that
my heart was *in* much of what I got up to in these "trashy years" . . .'
I.H. was forty-five in 1983. Line 3, 'He must have asked himself': cf.
'Dockery and Son' by Philip Larkin: 'Dockery, now: / Only nineteen,
he must have taken stock / Of what he wanted . . .' etc. See the Introduction, also 'Biography' (p.63) and note; and I.H.'s review-essay of
1995, 'Edmund Wilson's Wounds'.

53 'House Work': First published in *Agenda*, Winter/Spring 1987.

54 'The Garden': First published in *The London Review of Books*, July
1990. I.H.'s poem bears at most an oblique relation to its celebrated
predecessor by Andrew Marvell; but lines 1 and 2, '. . . green-shadowed
/ Shadowed green': cf. Marvell, 'The Garden' ('. . . Annihilating all
that's made / To a green thought in a green shade'), 'Bermudas' ('He

lands us on a grassy stage . . . golden lamps in a green night'); and 'The Mower's Song':

> My mind was once the true survey
> Of all these meadows fresh and gay,
> And in the greenness of the grass
> Did see its hopes as in a glass

etc. From Dante onwards, green has frequently signified hope, whether worldly hope or hope of salvation; and in colloquial speech it can still connote freshness or innocence. (It carries something of these meanings in several poems of I.H.'s: see 'Now and Then', 'Anniversary', 'New Year', 'Dream Song'; but also 'The Forties'.) Line 4, 'Some cobbled little serpent of a path': the serpent makes its appearance in the Garden of Eden in the Book of Genesis, 3:1. Line 15, 'Lay down your scythe': cf., again, Marvell's 'Mower' poems, especially 'The Mower Against Gardens' and 'Damon the Mower':

> Sharp like his scythe his sorrow was,
> And withered like his hopes the grass [. . .]

> 'But now I all the day complain,
> Joining my labour to my pain;
> And with my scythe cut down the Grass
> Yet still my grief is where it was . . .' etc.

55 'Again': First published in the *London Review of Books*, July 1990.

56 'At Evening': First published in the *London Review of Books*, July 1990.

57 'Soliloquy': First published in the *London Review of Books*, July 1990.

58 'Steps': First published in the *London Review of Books*, August 1995; also the title of the booklet published in 1997. Line 1, 'Where do we find ourselves . . .'etc: adapted from the beginning of an essay, 'Experience' (1844) by Ralph Waldo Emerson (1803–82): 'Where do we find ourselves? In a series of which we do not know the extremes, and believe that it has none. We wake and find ourselves on a stair; there are stairs below us, which we seem to have ascended; there are stairs above us, many a one, which go upward and out of sight. But the Genius which, according to the old belief, stands at the door by which we enter, and gives us the lethe to drink, that we may tell no tales, mixed the cup too strongly, and we cannot shake off the lethargy now at noonday. Sleep lingers all our lifetime about our eyes, as night hovers all day in the boughs of the fir-tree.' Matthew Arnold, the subject of I.H.'s last biography, was reading Emerson in the 1840s, and wrote

or drafted his poem 'Written in Emerson's Essays' in 1844. Arnold's poem 'adds the American's "voice oracular" to those other Oxford "voices in the air"'; here, thought Arnold, was a voice '"as new and moving and unforgettable as the strains of Newman, or Carlyle or Goethe"': I.H., *A Gift Imprisoned: The Poetic Life of Matthew Arnold* (1998).

59 'Fever': First published in the *London Review of Books*, August 1995.

60 'Resolve': First published in the *London Review of Books*, August 1995. In several typewritten drafts this poem is titled 'Bad Muse'. Line 10, 'Enchantress, know-all . . .' etc.: cf. A. E. Housman, *Last Poems*, xl:

> Tell me not here, it needs not saying,
>   What tune the enchantress plays
> In aftermaths of soft September
>   Or under blanching ways,
> For she and I were long acquainted
>   And I knew all her ways

and iii:

> Her strong enchantments failing [. . .]
>
> O Queen of air and darkness
>   I think 'tis truth you say,
> And I shall die tomorrow;
>   But you will die today.

Line 15, 'Let's call this . . .' etc.: cf. 'Almost Nothing', p.65 and note, and 'Spring', p.85 and note.

61 'Dream Song': First published in the *London Review of Books*, March 1989. *The Dream Songs* by John Berryman, originally published in two volumes (*77 Dream Songs*, 1964, and *His Toy, His Dream, His Rest*, 1968), constitute one of the most original and distinctive achievements of post-war American poetry. I.H. was severe on *77 Dream Songs* in his review-essays 'Songs Among the Ruins' and 'John Berryman' (both 1965), but he qualified this severity when he wrote on Berryman many years later in *Against Oblivion*. In the interim, several of the Songs were first published by I.H. in his capacity as poetry editor of the *Times Literary Supplement*, and critical appreciations of Berryman appeared in *The Review* and *The New Review*. With very few exceptions, each Dream Song consists of eighteen irregularly-rhymed lines in three six-line stanzas; Hamilton's poem extends this

template by one line. Lines 1 and 2, 'He called you Master of beauty, / Craftsman of the snowflake': the reference is not to a Dream Song but to the opening of a sequence, 'Eleven Addresses To the Lord', from Berryman's *Love & Fame* (1970), the book that followed *His Toy, His Dream, His Rest*. Most of the poems in *Love & Fame* deal with Berryman's late-reawakened Christian faith and treatment for alcoholism, which is also the material of his unfinished novel *Recovery*, published posthumously in 1973. (Berryman committed suicide in 1972; a final volume of poems, *Delusions, Etc.*, also appeared posthumously that year.) See the drafts of I.H.'s unpublished poem 'Letter to the Editor' (1988: Appendix 1, p.115), also 'Prayer', p.88; and the Introduction.

62 'Responsibilities': First published in the *London Review of Books*, March 1989. See note to 'In Dreams', above, and the Introduction.

63 'Biography': First published in the *London Review of Books*, August 1995. Line 4, The Middle Years: the title of a story by Henry James (1843–1916), published in 1893, in which a dying novelist, convinced that he has come, too late, to artistic maturity, longs for a 'second chance', a second creative life. It was also to have been the title of James's third volume of autobiography, and was in fact the title given to the third volume of Leon Edel's five-volume Life of James (1953–72). It is to this last, and to the relation of biography and biographers to writers' lives in general, that the poem principally refers. Line 5, 'Now look at him': 'Whenever we "meet on the broad highway the rueful denuded figure" of an eminent biographee, we recognise that "mystery has fled with a shriek". We also note that it is always as if the biographee has been taken by surprise, as if some unforeseen, unforeseeable accident has taken place': I.H., quoting James in chapter twelve of *Keepers of The Flame: Literary Estates and the Rise of Biography, from Shakespeare to Plath*, 1992. Edel also edited four volumes of Edmund Wilson's journals; see 'The Forties', p.52, and note; and the Introduction.

64 'Family Album': First published in the *London Review of Books*, April 2001.

65 'Almost Nothing': First published in the *London Review of Books*, April 2001. Line 18, 'I'll call it . . .' etc: cf. 'Resolve', p.60 and note; and 'Spring', p.85 and note.

69 'Your Place': Published in the Oxford student magazine *The New University*, No. 8, 1961. Uncollected. The 'great slow fish' is perhaps a

variation on an image in 'Behaviour of Fish in an Egyptian Tea Room' by Keith Douglas:

> As a white stone draws down the fish
> she on the seafloor of the afternoon
> draws down men's glances and their cruel wish
> for love

etc. Douglas (1920–44) served as a tank commander in the North African desert and was killed soon after the D-Day landings in Normandy. A generous selection of his poems was included in *The Poetry of War 1939–1945*, an anthology edited by I.H. (1965). In his essay 'The Forties' (1964), I.H. says that with 'the gay inventiveness' of 'Behaviour of Fish . . .' Douglas had 'come close to finding his true voice'. In the same essay he quotes from one of Douglas's letters to J. C. Hall, in which Douglas responds to criticism of his work as insufficiently lyrical: 'A lyric form and a lyric approach will do even less good than a journalese approach to the subjects we have to discuss now. I don't know whether you have come across the word Bullshit – it is an army word and signifies humbug and unnecessary detail. It symbolizes what I think must be got rid of – the mass of irrelevancies, of "attitudes", "approaches", propaganda, ivory towers, etc. . . . My object (and I don't give a damn about my duty as a poet) is to write true things, significant things in words each of which works for its place in the line . . .' I.H. cited the same letter almost forty years later in a review of Douglas's *Letters* (2001), and a third and final time in his chapter on Douglas in *Against Oblivion* (2002). See the Introduction; also 'The Veteran', p.74, and note below.

70 'Parting': Published in *The New University*, No. 8, 1961. Uncollected.

71 'Us and Flies': Published in the *Times Literary Supplement*, May 1961. Uncollected. Compare the flies with those in 'The Recruits' (p.7 and note) and 'Windfalls' (p.8 and note). Cf. also Shakespeare, *King Lear*, 4. 1: 'As flies to wanton boys, are we to the gods: / They kill us for their sport'.

72 'Fears': Published in *Oxford Opinion*, May 1961, and in the *Observer*, January 1962 (where it read 'You tell that ghosts . . .', and was divided into three parts, line 10 isolated with one line space above and below); and in *Pretending Not to Sleep*. Not published again. Cf. 'Trucks', p.6, and 'Apology', p.73.

73 'Apology': Published thus in *Universities Poetry 4*, April 1962. As pub-

lished in *Stand* (Leeds), 5/2, 1962, the poem is divided into four tercets; in that form it is (very) slightly suggestive of poems by Keith Douglas and William Empson that I.H. admired. Uncollected.

74 'The Veteran': Cyclostyled typescript, 1962. Unpublished. This 'grey, hard-veined old ruin' is surely a veteran of the First World War rather than the Second – since most who saw active service in 1939–45 would only have been in their forties or at most their fifties when this poem was written, in the early 1960s. All the same, his attitude of 'contempt' represents something important and ungainsayable. *The Poetry of War 1939–45*, edited by I.H., includes a series of prose statements by poets about their wartime service, and in his introduction I.H. comments, 'I trust that these [statements] will compensate for whatever seems too literary and speculative in my own approach to the period these poets lived through.' The anthology gives prominence to Roy Fuller, to Keith Douglas (see note to 'Your Place', above) and, even more to Alun Lewis, whose more lyrical and expansive poems of the war suggest the conflicts of a romantic sensibility under duress. In his essay 'The Forties' I.H. writes, 'If what one misses in Douglas, finally, is the sense of a firm, discovered personality, there is no such problem with Alun Lewis, the most directly confessional of the important war poets.' See also the introduction to *Alun Lewis: Selected Poetry and Prose*, edited by I.H., and the chapter on Lewis in *Against Oblivion*.

75 'The Silence': (?) 1960s. I.H. typescript. Unpublished. The silence, the hands, the placing of 'Your words' all belong with the poems of *The Visit* while the walk, the countrified setting, the branch and snow look forward to the poems that would subsequently appear in *Returning* (cf. 'Anniversary', p.44).

76 'The Birds': (?) 1960s. I.H. typescript. Unpublished. The poem seems indebted to the 1963 film of the same name by Alfred Hitchcock, adapted from a story by Daphne du Maurier.

77 'Vigil': First published by the Poem of the Month Club, 1971 ; then in *The Review*, 29/30, Spring–Summer 1972 (the final number of the magazine), and in *Returning*, but not thereafter. In conversation with Peter Dale (published in *Agenda*, Vol. 31 No. 2, 1993), I.H. commented: 'You could say that [*The Review*] was a victim of its own stringency, of its insistence that good poems happened very rarely . . . [It] had its own destruction built into it. *The Review* poems tended more and more towards the aphoristic, the epigrammatic and so on. They

weren't taking on dramatic or narrative challenges or even much of an emotional challenge; in the end they were just admiring their own brevity. And that's really why it stopped.'

78 'Fair': Published in *The Humanist* (US), March–April 1973. Uncollected. This seems a poem on determinedly Imagist lines, but an undated holograph version concludes:

> We are young mothers
> One day older now, and happily
> One long day nearer home.

Cf. 'Afternoons' by Philip Larkin:

> In the hollows of afternoons
> Young mothers assemble
> At swing and sandpit
> Setting free their children

etc. See note to 'Vigil' above.

79 'Untranslatable': (?) 1970s/80s. I.H. typescript. Unpublished. The first three lines adapt the opening of 'Necessary Explanation', the poem that introduces *Poems of Yannis Ritsos, in English versions by Alan Page*, a pamphlet published by *The Review*: No. 21 Part 3, 1969 (Parts 1 and 2 were poems by Colin Falck and Hugo Williams, respectively. Alan Page, an exact contemporary of I.H., attended Darlington Grammar School with him.) Robert Frost famously defined poetry as 'what gets lost in translation'; I.H.'s *ars poetica* implicitly endorses the (quoted) speaker's fascination with the 'untranslatable', with meanings that are mysterious or elusive, that cannot be pinned down or paraphrased. In conversation I.H. acknowledged the haunting effect of 'certain lines' and 'whole poems, even' that resist paraphrase and explication – by, for example, William Empson, whose 'Missing Dates' ('The waste remains, the waste remains and kills') he often quoted admiringly, but about whose poetry he was otherwise sceptical. 'Untranslatable' is also a comment, perhaps, on some poetic careers more given over to 'expansiveness' and 'bulk' than Hamilton's was: see the Introduction, and his preface to *Fifty Poems* in Appendix 3.

80 'Work in Progress': 1980s/90s. Published in *The Poetry Book Society Anthology 3*, ed. William Scammell; London, 1992. Line 5 in the published version reads '. . . typography incurably diseased' and the final lines read 'And on the sleeve, his photograph: / He's felling trees'. A

later ts. has been preferred here. (Another ts and a holograph copy – not I.H.'s – have the alternative title 'Country Cousin'.) Line 1, 'breathologist': in his essay 'All-American' (1964), I.H. wrote of the legacy of William Carlos Williams: 'Williams's reputation in the United States is currently at its height and . . . all really ambitious American experimenters are breaking their lines in accordance to strange, secret dictates from the breath and the pulse-rate'. He returned to this theme in his chapter on Williams in *Against Oblivion*, where he elaborated, 'On the page, the effect is as one might expect: staccato, broken, short of wind'. Lines 3-4, 'a slim vol / Entitled: *Big*': in his interview with Dan Jacobson I.H. recalls undertaking a reading tour of the United States in 1973, in the course of which he visited the poet and bestselling novelist James Dickey: 'He played blue-grass music and he had this lake on his property and was forever showing off his muscles and thighs. At one point he said, "Yes, I'm so big, I'm so goddam big! And no cocksucking English critic's gonna tell me any different!" . . . You passed this table [in his house] where all his publications were set out on display. "Yeah, my pamphlet, preddy good, ha." . . . When I left he gave me a rib-crushing bear-hug and there were tears running down his face. "Oh, it's been so *good*," he said . . . When I looked back he was leaning against his doorpost, his head in his hands, as if he'd just lost his nearest and dearest. And I'd only been there two hours. But that poet had big emotions.' Though owing something, obviously, to Dickey, the American poet here is probably a composite figure from different episodes in I.H.'s 'so-called literary life', of which this poem, along with 'An Alternative Agenda' (p.81), affords us a rare glimpse. See the Introduction, and Appendix 3.

81 'An Alternative Agenda': Published in the *London Review of Books*, June 1987. Uncollected. Karl Miller (author and literary critic, Lord Northcliffe Professor of Modern English Literature, University College London, 1974–92, and Editor of the *LRB*, 1979–92), Jeremy Treglown (Editor, the *Times Literary Supplement*, 1982–90, biographer, and Professor of English at the University of Warwick since 1993) and Peter Porter (poet, freelance writer and broadcaster, b. 1929 in Brisbane, Australia, and resident in London from 1951) all accompanied I.H. to a conference on literary journals in Canberra in May, 1987. In his essay 'Litfest in Oz' (1983), I.H. had written about an earlier trip to Australia, in the 1970s: 'The Adelaide festival was prefaced by a "forum" of little magazine editors (that is to say, editors of

so-called Little Magazines). I was then editing *The New Review* and was thus the foreign guest who was supposed to give the Australians an idea of how we handled these things here. Once the event got going, though, it swiftly became clear that how we handled these things here was of no interest whatever to the dozen or so tense figures round the table. Each of them had something on his mind, something very local and specific, and each was determined to be heard . . . Among poets there was much talk of an "Australian identity"; one way of asserting that identity was to be indifferent to anything that was going on in London'.

85 'Spring': (?) 1980s / 90s. I.H. typescript. Unpublished. Line 8, 'Let's call it . . .' etc: see 'Resolve', p.60, and 'Almost Nothing', p.65. Successive drafts of 'Early Work', an unfinished poem from late in I.H.'s life, end '. . . it's pleasure / But let's call it work, let's call it early work'.

86 'Negatives': 1988. I.H. typescript. Unpublished. See note to 'Larkinesque', above.

87 'Ties': (?) 1980s / 90s. I.H. typescript. Unpublished. As well as two clean typescripts (one struck through in pen), there is one with autograph alterations, some of them cancelled, to line 4. It is not possible to establish the chronological order of the TSS or exactly what I.H.'s intentions were, or to consider this poem 'finished', but of the alternatives the version here has the strongest claim. It is remarkable, apart from anything else, for containing the unique instance in I.H.'s work of explicit allusion to Thomas Hardy, a poet to whom he felt deeply indebted. Line 4, 'And anyway, white storm birds sing no song': cf.

> They clear the creeping moss –
> Elders and juniors – aye,
> Making the pathways neat
>   And the garden gay;
> And they build a shady seat . . .
>   Ah, no; the years, the years;
> See, the white storm-birds wing across!

– a stanza from Hardy's 'During Wind and Rain'. Line 8, 'His, yours, theirs . . .' echoes the refrains, 'He, she, all of them, yea', in the first and final stanzas of the same poem. I.H.'s selection from Hardy for Bloomsbury Poetry Classics was published in 1992. In the late 1980s and early '90s he was preoccupied with literary posterity, writers' estates and 'afterfame', the subjects of his book *Keepers of the Flame*, which includes a chapter on Hardy and his second marriage. Soon after Hardy's death, his widow Florence published a Life of her husband under her own name, though it had largely been written by him. In *Keepers* I.H. quotes from one of Florence's letters written soon after the publication of *Satires of Circumstance*, containing Hardy's 'Poems of 1912-13' – elegies for his first wife, Emma, in which grief and tenderness are inextricable from regret and remorse: 'It seems to me that I am an utter failure if my husband can publish such a *sad sad* book ... I cannot get rid of the feeling that the man who wrote some of these poems is utterly weary of life – and cares for nothing in this world'. I.H. remarried in 1981. Among his papers from this period is a fragment consisting of some lines of 'Ties' but with the title 'Second Wife'.

88 'Prayer': (?) 1980s / 90s. I.H. typescripts. Unpublished. Given I.H.'s lifelong tendency to cut and condense, it is reasonable to assume that 'Prayer' is the final, drastic recension of a – similarly unpublished – poem of very different import, called 'Letter to the Editor' (1988), several drafts of which were among I.H.'s papers. (See Appendix 1. This poem was itself cut down to nineteen lines from an initial thirty-five.) From another typescript with autograph alterations (see below) it is clear that 'Prayer' was taken up again, and changes were made, at what would seem to have been a very late stage in I.H.'s life.

> Look sir, my hands are steady now,
> My brain a cloudless [~~day~~] sky.
> Is that the sound of breakfast down below?
> To eat again seems possible.
> To breathe?
> No problem, Lord, [~~I promise.~~] [~~I'm OK.~~] [~~I'll try~~]. But why?

Appendix 1

Letter to the Editor

A poem in several typewritten drafts, with autograph revisions; 1988.
(Unpublished; ?unfinished.)

[A]

My hand seemed steady,
Steadier, my brain
Near-cloudless. I could hear
Faint kitchen-sounds below.
To eat seemed possible.
To breathe
No problem, Lord:
The customary hiss
But not so guttural,
No cough.
I think I even thought
Thank God, one of those
Better days
I haven't had a taste of since –
Well, you would know.

By now you will have read
My manuscript, my text
My thanks to you
Delirious Last Will:
'To die, to cease, perchance
To dream upon the midnight
With no pain, and in that dream
Perchance to supplicate . . .'
And so it went. But Lord, **N.B**
[N. B.] Please let it not,
O let it not be said
That nothing, not a [squeak] **syllable**, (?)
A semi-syllable,
A sigh,

Can yet be salvaged from
This you would say
This winking of an eye,
This grain of sand,
This life-time's wreck of speech,
This haunting.

[B]

My hand seemed steady,
Steadier, my brain
Near-cloudless. I could hear
Faint kitchen-sounds below.
To eat seemed possible.
To breathe
No problem, Lord:
The customary hiss
But not so guttural,
No cough.
I think I even thought:
Thank God, one of those
Better days
I haven't had a taste of since –
Well, you would know.

By now you will have read
My manuscript, my text
My thanks to you
Delirious Last Will:
'To die, to cease, perchance
To dream upon the midnight
With no pain, and in that dream
Perchance to supplicate . . .'
And so it went. But Lord, N. B.
Please let it not,
O let it not be said
That nothing, not a syllable,
A semi-syllable,
A sigh,
Can yet be salvaged from
This life-time's wreck of speech,
This haunting.

[C]

My hand seemed steady,
Steadier, my brain
Near-cloudless. I could hear
Faint kitchen-sounds below.
To eat seemed possible.
To breathe
No problem, Lord:
The customary hiss
But not so guttural,
No cough.
I think I even thought:
Thank God, one of those
Better days
I haven't had a taste of since…
Well, you would know.

By now you will have seen
My manuscript,
My thanks to you
Delirious Last Will:
'To die, to cease, perchance
To dream upon the midnight
With no pain and in that dream
Perchance to supplicate . . .'
And so it went. Delirium. But Lord,
Please let it not **be said**
[O let it not be said]
That nothing, not a syllable,
A semi-syllable,
A sigh,
Can yet be salvaged from
This life-time's wreck of speech,
This haunting.

[D]

My hand seemed steady,
Steadier, my brain
Near-cloudless. I could hear
Faint kitchen-sounds below.
To eat seemed possible;
To breathe: no problem, Lord:
The customary hiss
But not so guttural,
No cough.
Thank God, one of those
Better days
I haven't had a taste of since . . .
Well, you would know.

By now you will have seen
My manuscript,
My thanks to you
Delirious Last Will:
'To die, to cease, perchance
Upon the midnight
With no pain and in that dream
Perchance to supplicate . . .'
And so it went. Delirium. But Lord,
Please let it not be said
That nothing, not a syllable,
A semi-syllable, a sigh,
Can yet be salvaged from
This life-time's wreck of speech,
This haunting.

[E]

My hand seemed steady,
Steadier, my brain
Near-cloudless. I could hear
Faint kitchen-sounds below.
To eat seemed possible;
To breathe: no problem, Lord;
The customary hiss
But not so guttural,
No cough.
Thank God, one of those
Better days
I haven't had a taste of since . . .
[Well you would know.] But Lord,

By now you will have seen
My manuscript,
My thanks to you
Delirious Last Will:
'To die, to cease, perchance
Upon the midnight
With no pain and in that dream
Perchance to supplicate . . .'
And so it went. Delirium. [But Lord,]
Please let it not be said
That nothing, not a syllable,
A semi-syllable, [a sigh]
Can yet be salvaged from
This life-time's wreck of speech,
This haunting.

[F]

Letter to the Editor

My hand seemed steady,
Steadier, my brain
Near-cloudless. I could hear
Faint kitchen-sounds below.
To eat seemed possible;
To breathe: no problem, Lord;
The customary hiss
But not so guttural,
No cough.
Thank God, one of those
Better days
I haven't had a taste of since . . .
But Lord,
Please let it not be said
That nothing, not a syllable,
A semi-syllable,
Can yet be salvaged from
This life-time's wreck of speech,
This haunting.

Appendix 2

1 'Strange Meeting', by 'Edward Pygge' (and I.H. on traditional forms and free verse)

Strange Meeting

Swollen with booze and bursting for a pee
Hither I came to seek the easing spring.
Said barman Sam: 'I think you'll find it's free
In there, ducks.' But I couldn't see a thing

At first and merely groped towards the wall
Impatiently. No reassuring trough
Revealed itself, no friendly waterfall
Embraced my urgent boots. Instead, a cough

Rang out and turning wildly I could see,
Flanked by two huge incinerators, Sam
Renowned for milds and bitters! Lustfully
He eyed my poignant zip and cried: 'Poor lamb

You really didn't know that here in Hades
All our lovely loos are labelled 'Ladies'?'

Edward Pygge

'Strange Meeting', a (Shakespearean) sonnet, won a *New Statesman* Weekend Competition (No. 2,004; 9 August 1968) which invited readers to 'comment in sonnet form' on a letter that had appeared in the *Sun*, ending 'All our lovely loos . . .' etc., using this formula as either the first or the last line. 'Edward Pygge' was the *nom de guerre* first adopted by I.H. – sometimes working in collaboration with John Fuller or Colin Falck – for reviews and parodies of contemporaries that appeared in *The Review*. (The 'Edward Pygge' byline survived that magazine, and those later writing under it included Julian Barnes, Clive James, Russell Davies and Craig Raine.) Replying to an enquiry from the bibliographer Ryan Roberts, I.H. commented of this poem, 'I was pretty proud of it at the time.'

'Strange Meeting': the title of a poem by Wilfred Owen (1893–1918) which imagines an encounter in Hell between an English soldier of the First World War and the German 'enemy' he has killed.

Lines 1–2, 'Swollen . . . spring': cf. 'Twicknam Garden', by John Donne (1572–1631), which begins 'Blasted with sighs, and surrounded with teares / Hither I come to seeke the Spring . . .'

Neither of these 'precursors' is a sonnet. In an interview with Gerry Cambridge published in *The Dark Horse*, No. 3, Hamilton spent some time discussing the implications, for him, of 'traditional forms'. Asked if his ideas about inspiration meant that 'setting out to write a poem in formal stanzas is not something [he] would ever try', Hamilton replied: 'I have done that type of thing, but for satirical purposes. I'm very interested in rhymes and half-rhymes; all my poems have some sort of iambic base to them . . . That's the sound in my head. But if that sound had been a bit more regular I would have feared that that regularity of sound implied some regularity of thought; in other words, that I knew what I was talking about, and what I wanted to say. I think modern poetry has backed away from traditional metres because of a general loss of belief and philosophical certainty. The idea of shapeliness and regularity in poetry has been dissonant with loss of belief and with general scepticism, which of course needn't be the case . . . I think that that deep and rich familiarity with [the sonnet], that you can write in it self-expressively, without technical self-consciousness, which must have been true in the early nineteenth century – otherwise you wouldn't have some of Keats's sonnets – has been largely lost. The form is so distant now and so exotic . . . Until the New Formalists, the only people who habitually wrote in tight metres would be light-versifiers, which implied some sort of levity or detachment. Though you have to exempt Auden. But I've never felt particularly moved by a poem of Auden's. It's to do almost with a cocksureness in his use of strict forms. He's almost saying: *I have controlled my experience as I am controlling this. I am in charge of me, I know who I am, I know the rules, and I can perform.* So questions of tentativeness, uncertainty, anguish – there's no place for them. His persona is that of a man who knows how to speak in traditional forms. The speaking voice in some Lowell poems is that of a man who doesn't know how to speak. He doesn't know how it's going to turn out when he starts speaking – though of course he does, it's just an illusion. But the persona he *projects* is of uncertainty, whereas the poet of traditional forms projects the persona of certainty – you might say . . . Larkin is so interesting because he managed to write in such strict metres, with such interest in rhyme schemes, without any diminution of personal sorrow or intensity. That used to make me marvel: how do you do this, how do you perform so skilfully while at the same time managing to project such hopelessness?' And at one point in his conversations with Dan Jacobson, Hamilton says, 'I sometimes wish I'd been a different sort of poet [but] the poems I've produced happened to be the only things I could do. I've certainly tried other things, many exercises, and I've tried to write sonnets and tried to write quatrains. I could do all of that quite fluently but I never thought it was poetry. I thought of it as verse. It had no power of the kind that made me respond to poetry in the first place.'

11 On Dylan Thomas and the Movement

I.H.'s feelings about his early enthusiasms, for example Dylan Thomas (1914–53), and about the poets of the 1950s who dominated his undergraduate years, were complex, and changed over time. A reaction to the former set in fairly soon after the initial attraction; and something similar had occurred concerning the latter (if attraction there had ever been) by 1971, when in an essay, 'The Making of the Movement', I.H. took unforgiving aim at the poets who came to prominence with D. J. Enright's *Poets of the 1950s* and Robert Conquest's *New Lines*: 'The Movement, along with the Sitwells, has its distinctive niche in the history of publicity . . . neatly tailored ironies . . . feeble neo-Augustan posturings . . . effortful Empsonian pastiche . . . Today . . . it seems difficult to conceive of aridity more notable than theirs . . . Poems-as-criticism, or as literary journalism . . . each inhabits an imaginative world dominated by trivial exigencies of literary warfare . . ', etc. (An exception was made, of course, for Philip Larkin.) By 1993, in his interview with Peter Dale in *Agenda* (Vol. 31, No. 2: 'The Sixties Reconsidered'), he saw the conflict in more subtle and more moderate terms:

IH: I remember being bowled over, thrilled by Dylan Thomas when I was sixteen or seventeen. I began writing dreadful Dylan Thomas-type poems. And later on, after repudiating Thomas, I wanted to recapture that Thomas-type excitement, to find something like it in the anti-Thomas poems I then began arguing for: these new, clear, disciplined poems of the future. However bad Thomas was, he did, at that age, have a lot of glamour and excitement.

PD: Yes. I did read a lot of Thomas, then, too . . . I felt, reading him, that poetry was something important, that it mattered. And, going back to Pound, I had the same feeling with him: here was a man who believed that poetry was vital. You didn't get that feeling from the Movement.

IH: Yes, but it was hard in the early sixties to stand up and say 'poetry is important' without sounding like a throwback to the forties. The Movement had that effect. In 1962, you would rather have been like Larkin than like Dylan Thomas. But you didn't want to be like Larkin either. There was something very attractive about the Larkin-Amis debunking but there was also something it missed out on, something one prized but could not name – not without embarrassment, not without some Movement-inspired fear of sounding arty and pretentious. One was torn. So one stuck to what felt genuine – poems about personal experience, poems that made no great emotional gestures but were 'feelingful'.

PD: Two prose writers, Orwell and Salinger, were influences both on the Movement and on *The Review*. Phoniness was the great fear.

IH: Yes and then anti-phoniness turned into a new sort of phoniness: the poet as ordinary guy.

I.H. and P.D. also touch on the importance, to the young Hamilton and *The Review*, of Ezra Pound's Imagist precepts, and the disagreement over Pound (as over much else) between A. Alvarez and Donald Davie published in the first number of the magazine, in 1962. To Alvarez, I.H. recalled, Pound was 'an art man', and what Alvarez wanted in poetry was more 'life'; for the poets and critics of *The Review*, if a poet could 'inject some Alvarez-type "life"' into poems that simultaneously obeyed Pound's 'art principles', 'you might', according to I.H., 'get something rather wonderful.'

Appendix 3

1 Contents of I.H.'s books of poetry

Pretending Not to Sleep (*The Review*, 1964)

Fears; The Storm; Windfalls; The Recruits; Trucks; A Mother's
Complaint; Father, Dying; Birthday Poem; Metaphor; Last Illness;
Last Respects; The Funeral; Pretending Not to Sleep; Poem (To G)

The Visit (Faber, 1970)

The Storm; Pretending Not to Sleep; Trucks; The Recruits;
Windfalls; Bequest; Father, Dying; Birthday Poem; Metaphor; Last
Illness; Last Respects; Funeral; Epitaph; Complaint; Night Walk;
Poem; Admission; Last Waltz; Home; Memorial; The Visit; The Vow;
Your Cry; Awakening; Aftermath; Nature; Words; Old Photograph;
Neighbours; Breaking Up; Newscast; Curfew; Now and Then

Returning (privately printed, 1976)

Vigil; Ghosts; Retreat; Critique; Poet; Bedtime Story; Friends; In
Dreams; Anniversary; Rose; Returning; Remember This

Fifty Poems (Faber, 1988)

Memorial; The Storm; Pretending Not to Sleep; Trucks; The Recruits;
Windfalls; Birthday Poem; Metaphor; Father, Dying; Bequest;
Midwinter; Last Respects; Funeral; Epitaph; Complaint; Night Walk;
Poem; Admission; Last Waltz; Nature; Home; The Visit; The Vow;
Your Cry; Awakening; Aftermath; Words; Old Photograph;
Neighbours; Breaking Up; Newscast; Curfew; Now and Then; Retreat;
Friends; In Dreams; Bedtime Story; Poet; Critique; Ghosts; Rose;
Anniversary; Returning; Remember This; New Year; Colours;
Familiars; Larkinesque; House Work; The Forties

Steps (Cargo Press, 1997)

The Garden; Again; At Evening; Soliloquy; Steps; Fever; Resolve;
Dream Song; Responsibilities; Biography

Sixty Poems (Faber, 1998)

Memorial; The Storm; Pretending Not to Sleep; Trucks; The Recruits;
Windfalls; Birthday Poem; Metaphor; Father, Dying; Bequest;
Midwinter; Last Respects; Funeral; Epitaph; Complaint; Night Walk;
Poem; Admission; Last Waltz; Nature; Home; The Visit; The Vow;
Your Cry; Awakening; Aftermath; Words; Old Photograph;
Neighbours; Breaking Up; Newscast; Curfew; Now and Then; Retreat;
Friends; In Dreams; Bedtime Story; Poet; Critique; Ghosts; Rose;
Anniversary; Returning; Remember This; New Year; Colours;
Familiars; Larkinesque; The Forties; House Work; The Garden;
Again; At Evening; Soliloquy; Steps; Fever; Resolve; Dream Song;
Responsibilities; Biography

11 Ian Hamilton writes . . .

Poetry Book Society *Bulletin*, No. 65: Summer 1970

The poems in *The Visit* were written between 1962 and 1969 and are
printed in roughly chronological order. They are all, at some level,
autobiographical and they could all, I suppose, be described as
dramatic lyrics. That is to say, the reader is offered only the intense,
climactic moment of a drama – the prose part, the part which
provides the background data, is left to the imagination. The book,
as will readily be seen, falls into four sections or sequences, and yet
I would hope that if it is to be read straight through it will be read as
a kind of narrative.

   Not much elucidation is called for, I believe, but the following brief
notes may be worth something.

   'Pretending Not to Sleep: the 'characters' referred to in the first line
are derelicts who have cultivated the knack of sleeping in a sitting
position, so as not to be moved on.

   'Bequest': A dramatic monologue spoken by the father who is
addressed in subsequent poems.

   'Birthday Poem': The Empire Exhibition occurred in 1938, the year
in which the speaker in the poem had been born.

   'Awakening': One of several poems set in a mental hospital. The
woman addressed here is awakening after ECT, which impairs the
memory.

   'Last Waltz': The title refers to a hit song, ubiquitous at the time of
writing.

Preface to *Fifty Poems* (1988)

Fifty poems in twenty-five years: not much to show for half a life-time, you might think. And, in certain moods, I would agree. In certain moods, I used to crave expansiveness and bulk, and early on I had several shots at getting 'more of the world' into my verse: more narrative, more satire, more intelligence, and so on. Each time, however, I would end up knowing for certain that I could have tack-led the material more cogently in prose. Why push and strain?

And so I decided to stop thinking like a poetry pro, to stop fretting about 'range' and 'output'; decided, indeed, to keep the whole business of 'my poetry' quite separate from the rest of my so-called literary life: a life of book reviews, biographies, anthologies and magazines. I suppose I thought that I would wait for poetry to happen rather than force myself to go in search of it. After all, the poems I *had* written (this was *c.*1972) arrived more or less out of the blue, prompted by circumstance rather than by any subject-seeking impulse on my part.

The trouble with this line of thinking was that these 'out-of-the-blue' poems happened in my twenties; whenever I reread them, I could see that they were spoken in a voice that was no longer wholly mine: a voice made musical by a kind of anguished incredulity, a refusal to believe that fathers die, that wives go mad, that love – however certain of itself – is not enough, not always. But did I truly think that poetry, if perfect, could bring back the dead? In some way, yes, I think I did.

What strikes me now is that, although the poems I wrote in my twenties really do catch the tone and flavour of my life throughout the 1960s, I cannot say the same of the fifteen or so poems that came next. These later poems are written from the heart, but I'm not sure that my heart was *in* much of what I got up to in these 'trashy years' – from about 1973 to 1979. The raggedness of everything, the booze, the jokes, the literary feuds, the almost-love-affairs, the cash, the some-how getting-to-be-forty, and so on: where does all *that* show itself in these poems of my early middle-age? The answer is, it doesn't (well, not much). In fact, I'd now say that these later poems are bruised rewrites of what I'd done before. They are still, in this sense, poems of my youth.

I don't want to say anything about the very last poems in this book: I'm not certain what they signify nor how they connect up with the others. I think I feel (although I'd have a hard time backing this with names and dates) that if you are a lyric poet of the 'miraculous' persuasion, then you will never properly 'grow up'. There won't *be* a middle period of worldliness and commonsense – or if there is, you won't know what to do with it, in verse.

Index of Titles

Index of First Lines